NOT A SILENT PEOPLE:
CONTROVERSIES THAT HAVE SHAPED SOUTHERN BAPTISTS

NOT A SILENT PEOPLE

Controversies That Have Shaped Southern Baptists

Walter B. Shurden

BROADMAN PRESS/Nashville, Tennessee

The intent of this book is to present as objectively as is denominationally desirable a representative group of the major controversies that have shaped the Southern Baptist Convention. It is not the official statement of any polemical position but was commissioned to make a positive contribution toward understanding the lively tradition of a denomination the Lord has richly blessed. It is presented for reading in the light of its purpose.

Library of Congress Catalog Card Number: 79–178066
Dewey Decimal Classification Number: 286.09
Printed in the United States of America

Dedication

To Sherry, Paula, and Walt,
three good young ones
who have already learned that
controversy is part of the stuff of life.

Preface

My wife, reared a non-Baptist, was a bit taken back when she got an inside look into Baptist churches. The thing that struck her was the amount of fussin' and fightin' that goes on there. But to her it was a sign of life, of vitality, of concern. She declared on one occasion that she did not know that religious groups "cared enough to argue over anything." My response was, "If religious controversy is an index of how much people care, then Baptists care more than any group in the world."

Sometimes we Baptists have argued over major issues, and then again we have become vocal over trivia. But whether big or small, necessary or unnecessary, profitable or profitless, our denominational controversies have shaped us. We can't get away from their influence.

I really have three purposes for my Baptist readers. (If you are not a Baptist, I believe you will see the advantages of my writing directly to my brethren in this book.) One, I want to try to "turn Baptists on" to the denominational heritage. This means that I have tried to avoid the heavy hand of the historian. Pedantry is no virtue. And yet, for the historian, even pedantry is not as great a vice as inaccuracy. I wanted to avoid both. Two, I want to show how our Baptist past affects us today. And three, and more indirectly, I hope you find in these pages some reasons why you who are Baptist can be grateful for being so. (And, if you are not a Baptist, I hope you will find the following pages worth reading—for reasons that will become apparent later.)

Most of the following chapters were first published in *The Student* in a somewhat revised form during 1970–1971. I am grateful that Norman Bowman, editor of *The Student,* believes that our denominational heritage matters and that students ought to be exposed to it.

I have also had a good time sharing these pages with two local Baptist congregations. I taught these Baptist controversies in the College Department Sunday School at Broadway Baptist Church in Knoxville, Tennessee. This is supposed to be the "now" generation, bloated with the present, anti-historical, and all that. But I didn't find it to be true with these young people. Sherwood Baptist church of Albany, Georgia, also heard some of these addresses. It was my second visit to Sherwood to preach and teach history. They did me the pleasure of acting interested.

Three people are due thanks. W. Morgan Patterson, professor of church history at Southern Baptist Theological Seminary, and Claude L. Howe, Jr., professor of church history at New Orleans Baptist Theological Seminary, read the manuscript and made helpful suggestions. Of course they are not responsible for any mistakes I made. Kay, my wife, not only typed the manuscript, but stayed up late at night acting interested in the excerpts I read her from "old" Baptist books.

Nothing can be understood until you know its history. For that reason, the Baptist heritage matters. Someone asked Leon McBeth, Baptist church historian, "What have Baptists ever done that they should deserve a history?" So he wrote an article entitled, "Do Baptists Deserve a History?" Naturally he answered with a "yes." So do I.

WALTER B. SHURDEN

Contents

"Here Come the Battling Baptists"

I don't know who wrote it or when or where or what the circumstances were. But it reeks with pessimism. Hear the poem:

> Our fathers have been churchmen
> 1900 years or so
> And to every new suggestion
> They always answered no.

If you listen attentively in religious circles, you may hear less poetic versions of the same theme. I once heard a forty-five year old Baptist deacon say that the seven most famous words in Baptist churches were, "We never did it that way before." A student—one of those intelligent, talented kind who was in holy revolt against his religious upbringing—echoed the same song. He was stalking (and stalking *is* the words for this irate one) out of a Baptist Student Union State Convention. What the student described as a denominational "bigee" had just finished a rousing thirty minute sermon in which he called for allegiance to the status quo. It was after this that I heard the stalking one put the poetry into prose. "My! My! My!" he said, "The more things change, the more Baptists remain the same."

And I thought in the historical half of my mind: "Hasn't always been so!"

If you think that Baptists of today are devoted establishmentarians, if you see them as a herd of timid, effete, thumb-sucking Christians, fearful of any controversy and all change, I have two suggestions for you. One, you may be wrong, but this is not the place to argue that point. And two, even if you are right about the "now" Baptists, don't make the mistake of thinking that Baptists have always been domesticated.

Baptists were born in the bosom of radicalism! They are born fighters because they were born fighting. As a distinct denomination, Baptists first began in seventeenth-century England. Label the religious parties of that period and here is what you come up with: Anglicans (English Episcopalians) are the "conservatives"; Puritans are the "liberals"; Quakers, Congregationalists, and Baptists are the "radicals"! Think of that! Baptists were not among the conservatives, wanting to maintain status quo. They were not even among the avant garde liberals who wanted to tamper with the status quo and change it a little. They were among the radicals who wanted to *reverse* the religious establishment. That, reader friend, is a heady heritage! One that many Baptists have never learned. Or else it is one they learned and conveniently forgot. Either way, it is a tragic misuse of history.

Churches—like any type organization or society—are very much akin to children. Babies are eager for new experiences.

Unchained by crusty habits and molded attitudes, they are free and willing to try anything once! There was a time when Baptists were babies—flexible, open, courageous infants of God! They would try anything once—or so it seemed to their opposition.

I

You probably never will, but if someday during your leisure time you decide to write an historical essay on early Baptists, Gordon Kingsley has a suggestion for you; a good place to begin your research is in the records of court proceedings, search warrants, and prison records. Baptist names are writ large there. The seventeenth century in England was a virtual hurricane of political and religious change. It was a disordered society. And Baptists were looked upon "as chief culprits in the disorder of state and church." [1]

Baptists were the "agitators" of the seventeenth century. They were called, however, by even less complimentary names such as a "base sect," a "scab of error," a "seduced and . . . schismatical rabble of deluded children, servants, and people," "a profane and sacrilegious sect," "an impure and carnal sect," and like most who dare to question the sanctity of things-as-they are, Baptists were dubbed "anarchists." One of the opponents of our Baptist forefathers said that "if this sect prevaile, we shall have no Monarchie in the State, nor Hierarchie in the Church, but an Anarchie in both." [2] He made a mistake!

Could a group so maligned by people in high places be innocent? Just how many horns did our devilish ancestors have? And what was the nature of their sins? Being judged by their times, Baptists in both England and America during the 1600's could be accused of two gross errors. One was theological, the other was political. Both involved a heretical way of thinking and an obnoxious way of acting. Or so thought their adversaries.

Baptists were theological heretics because they dared to believe—and to say it out loud—that one could not be born or baptized into Christianity. *Christian discipleship is a style of living which involves choice—voluntary, conscious commitment.* That was the theological axiom from which Baptists developed. The implication was clear enough: infant baptism had to go! And not primarily because the infants were sprinkled. But because the infants were infants! Baptists' first concern regarding baptism was not the *mode* of baptism, whether immersion, sprinkling or pouring. Their first concern was the *subject* of baptism. But their concern that the subject of baptism be capable of consciously choosing to be baptized appeared as stark heresy to the tradition of infant baptism.

The Establishment (in this case, the Church of England) began to cry for "religious law and order." "You are destroying the Church of Christ and everything that is holy!" screamed the panic-stricken Anglicans. (You probably have observed, as did John W. Gardner,[3] that a common strategy for resisting the swirling currents of change is to stand on high moral ground and assert that the old way is bound up with what is moral and spiritual. That was the Anglican plan, too.) "Humbug," blurted back the Baptists, "we are not destroying the Church of Christ; we are restoring it!"

Baptists contended that to demand a regenerate church membership, made up of believers only, would not damage the church; it would only declare the real nature of the church. They therefore pulled out of the Church of England and became "dissenters," emphasizing a "gathered" rather than a "parish" church. A "gathered" church was made up of people who voluntarily united in Christian fellowship. One had to *decide* to join the gathered church. Not so with the parish church. One was a member of a parish church by virtue of involuntary baptism as an infant.

Describing the Baptists, one brilliant interpreter of Baptist life and thought said, "Their distinctive feature is the doctrine of the Church: that it must consist wholly of people who have pledged themselves to Christ Jesus." [4] That was Baptists' first instance of breaking with theological tradition, but it was certainly not the only place where they bucked the church fathers.[5]

By seventeenth-century ground rules, Baptists were far more than theological deviates; they were also political traitors. As a matter of fact, most Englishmen of this period considered theological dissent from the Church of England tantamount to political treason to the State of England. This was a scrambled-eggs society. Church and state came on the same plate and all mixed together! Baptists tried to unscramble the political-ecclesiastical eggs, maintaining that the State has no say-so over the soul of a man.

Some great free soul of history, who is yet anonymous to me, is supposed to have said something to the effect: "To cram a creed down a man's throat is rape of the soul!" Baptists agreed. But they went on to say that for the State to do the creed-cramming is to compound the assault. John Smyth, often called the first Baptist, spoke for all Baptists when he said, "The magistrate is not by vertue of his office to meddle with religion, or matters of conscience, to force and compell men to this or that form of religion." [6] Staid, starched citizens of merry ole England could hardly believe their ears. The authorities were being challenged.

Baptists did more than merely talk. They acted. *Baptists broke laws.* Deliberately, premeditatively, with full awareness of what they were doing—Baptists broke laws. They broke laws in England, and they broke laws in America. And they broke the laws because they felt them to be unjust laws. They broke them because they felt that there was a law which transcended civil law; it was the law of Scripture. So they refused to conform to civil statutes which curbed religious freedom.

Baptists paid for their protesting. No exaggeration, some bled. Some were publicly whipped. More than a few were imprisoned. All were buffetted with irrational name-calling. Society demanded order and obedience. Baptists responded that obedience is impossible and disorder inevitable when injustice prevails!

"Civil disobedience" was a popular phrase in America in the 1960's. But neither the term nor the idea is new. Our Baptist granddaddies cut their teeth on it and survived by it. Leon McBeth, Professor of Church History at Southwestern Seminary in Fort Worth, Texas, was exactly right when he said that some contemporary Baptists would be "scandalized to learn *how* our Baptist ancestors expressed their dissent against the establishment." [7] Nonconformity, theological and political, has long been a part of the Baptist vocabulary.

II

The Lutherans have Martin Luther. Presbyterians have

John Calvin. Methodists have John Wesley. But whom do Baptists have? Contrary to a popular belief, John the Baptist did not father us. We don't go back quite that far! Who then were our fathers? With what names do we personalize the Baptist heritage of nonconformity?

With John Smyth (Smith). As I said earlier, he is often called the first Baptist. Small wonder than that he was a religious refugee. Educated in the "liberal" tradition at Cambridge and an ordained Anglican, he proved himself a divisive man because of "personal preaching." This first Baptist-to-be was apparently socking it to the men of high places! So he lost his job! Wanting more fresh air for his soul than English atmosphere could provide, he scooted over to Holland. There he taught and preached what came to be known as basic Baptist distinctives.

John Smyth had a common name but that was the only ordinary thing about him. "He was extremely sensitive to new light and singularly fearless in acting upon his convictions, and was, therefore, often in advance of his age." [8] He is reputed to be the first Englishman to plead for full liberty of conscience. Ralph Sockman once described Jesus as a "conservative revolutionary" who "knew that the suction of what is behind is a greater deterrent than the resistance of what is ahead." [9] John Smyth apparently knew that, too. He constantly tried to escape the "suction of what is behind." In doing so, he spearheaded the Baptist tradition.

A close associate of John Smyth in Holland was another English refugee by the name of Thomas Helwys. Convinced that it was his duty to return to England and minister to his countrymen and because of some disagreements with Smyth, Helwys made his way back to his native land and organized a church at Spitalfields in 1612. This is often called the first Baptist congregation on English soil. Helwys' return to his native country was an act of religious faith. It was also political rashness. He was imprisoned. And he may have died behind bars.

Helwys is credited with the first English publication demanding universal religious liberty. "Let them be heretics, Turks, Jews or whatsoever," said Helwys, "it appertains not to the earthly power to punish them in the least measure." [10] The doctrine of full religious liberty, now so common and taken for granted, was then a perilous and fanatical concept. Helwys, a Baptist, was one of the leading fanatics.

III

One thing needs to be made clear about Smyth, Helwys and others of their stripe. They did not buck the establishment—culture, society, church, and state—just for the sake of raw, red-blooded rebellion. Theirs was no adolescent kicking of the traces just to hear the clanging and clonging. They rebelled because they had a vision of something worth saving. They rebelled against the concept of a "parish" church because they believed the idea of a "gathered" church was worth saving. They rebelled against a state enforced religion because they thought the freedom of the human spirit was worth saving. They rebelled against the priority of ecclesiastical institutionalism because they believed that the priority of the individual was worth saving.

C. S. Lewis described a character in one of his novels as having "a good deal of spaniel in him." Then Lewis added, "He liked to be liked." One can't read Baptist history without feeling that early Baptists wanted to be liked. They certainly

did not "like to be disliked." They started their denominational life with more maturity than that. But neither did
Baptists "like to be liked" enough to muffle conscience and
repress dissent. They therefore risked the agony of controversy and change.

"My! My! My! The more things change, the more Baptists
remain the same."

And I thought in the historical half of my mind: "Hasn't
always been so!"

NOTES

1. Gordon Kingsley, "Opposition to Early Baptists," (*Baptist
History and Heritage,* January, 1969) p. 19.

2. Daniel Featley, *The Dippers Dipt* (London, 1645) as quoted
in *Ibid.,* p. 26.

3. John W. Gardner, *Self-Renewal: The Individual and the In-
novative Society* (New York: Harper and Row, 1963) p. 49.

4. W. T. Whitley, *A History of British Baptists* (London: Charles
Griffin and Company, Limited, 1923) p. 4.

5. For further reading on early Baptist theology, see Earnest A.
Payne, *The Fellowship of Believers: Baptist Thought and Practice
Yesterday and Today;* H. Wheeler Robinson, *The Life and Faith of
the Baptists;* and Winthrop S. Hudson, editor, *Baptist Concepts of
the Church.*

6. As quoted in H. Wheeler Robinson, *The Life and Faith of the
Baptists* (London: The Kingsgate Press, 1946) p. 124.

7. Leon McBeth, "Do Baptists Deserve a History?", (*Home Missions,* January, 1970) p. 14.

8. A. C. Underwood, *A History of the English Baptists* (London:
The Carey Kingsgate Press Limited, 1947) pp. 44, 45.

9. Ralph W. Sockman, *The Paradoxes of Jesus* (New York: Abing-
don Press, 1936) p. 50.

10. As quoted in Underwood, p. 47.

The
"When Did Baptists Begin?"
Controversy
or
Baptists Argue About Their History

I don't know of a Southern Baptist church anywhere that has had an acute attack of enthusiasm about Baptist history. Do you? Take your church, for example. When was the last time you had some dry-as-dust speaker describe all the roots and branches of your denominational family tree? Announce a seminar on Baptist history and you have a mass exodus of church members looking for something "relevant" and "exciting."

"Let bygones be bygones" is the attitude of most Baptists toward their history. And that is o.k., except for the impossibility of it. Bygones are not *just* bygones. Our bygones are not has-beens. They are still with us, helping and short-changing us, damning and redeeming us, perverting and saving us. Bygones are present. They are present whether you know it or not, whether you care or not.

I

Baptists have not always—usually, but not always—ignored their past. In fact, one of the best brotherly blood-lettings Southern Baptists ever had was about Baptist history. By "best" blood-letting I mean Baptists got hot! I do not mean that it was good, though some good flowed from it. By "brotherly" blood-letting I mean Southern Baptists fought each other.

This fraternal fight over Baptist history is popularly called "the Whitsitt Controversy." Dr. W. H. Whitsitt, president and professor of Southern Baptist Theological Seminary in Louisville, Kentucky, was one of the charter members of that exclusive Southern Baptist group known as "The Friendless Fraternity of Exiled Professors." The tension got so tight that somebody had to go. Poor Professor Whitsitt! He was in the wrong place saying the right thing at the wrong time. It was his turn to exit. He waved goodby to Southern Seminary in 1899.

It is said that today one of the first so-called rules of life for faculty members on large university campuses is "Publish or Perish!" But for Dr. Whitsitt the slogan turned out to be "Publish *and* Perish!" Dr. Whitsitt published some articles and a book entitled *A Question in Baptist History* and he perished from Southern Seminary. But before he left, his writings created one of the most bitter and divisive controversies in all of Southern Baptist history.

What was it that Whitsitt said that stirred up such a hornets' nest? Why all the fuss? There were several issues involved, but basically it was an argument over the age of Baptists. Whitsitt crossed swords with a prevailing interpretation of Baptist history which said that Baptists had lived in unbroken succession since New Testament times. The overwhelming opinion among Baptist historians today is that Whitsitt waved the "sharpest" sword. Whitsitt was right. But dull swords can cause bleeding, too. Whitsitt bled, but won. Later historical investigations have supported his point of view. Contemporary Baptist historians in the six Southern Baptist theological seminaries continue to teach Whitsitt's point of view.

Whitsitt's point of view—what was it? He said that Baptists began in 1641 when they "recovered" the practice of believer's baptism by immersion in England and that it is historically inaccurate to trace the Baptist denomination back beyond that date. W. Morgan Patterson, a present-day church historian at Southern Seminary, said that Whitsitt "arrived at these conclusions after a thorough sifting of the primary sources and through the application of critical methodology." [1] That is one way of saying that Whitsitt had done his homework!

The historical error which Whitsitt wanted to correct was firmly entrenched in Southern Baptist life. It was merely assumed by most Baptists in the latter half of the nineteenth century that Baptists began in the year A.D. 30 and continued in unbroken succession. This Successionist Concept of Baptist History constitutes one of those ideas which enhances the position of a people and therefore goes unquestioned and unchallenged. The idea became a kind of Baptist sacred cow which one would touch or criticize at his peril. Successionism was too good not to be true, reasoned most Baptists.

The "Father of Baptist Church Succession" was an English Baptist minister by the name of G. H. Orchard. In 1823 he found himself in conversation with an Independent minister who maintained that Baptists were of recent historical origin. No historian, Orchard nevertheless refused to believe the minister and affirmed his confidence in the idea that Baptists had experienced a continuous existence "from the days of John the Baptists [sic], until now. . . ." [2] Immediately Orchard set out to prove his point by a study of church history.

Orchard is a perfect example of the fact that history can be terribly abused. As with the Bible, you can find what you want to find in history. Most religious denominations have! Orchard found what he was looking for by tracing the Baptist denomination back to the New Testament through all the dissenting movements in Christian history. In other words, most of those groups which dissented from Roman Catholicism were "Baptists" according to Orchard. (One contemporary Baptist writer aptly but facetiously dubbed this "the mole-hole theory of succession, linking us to Jerusalem, Jesus, and John the Baptist in unbroken continuity, sometimes under ground." [3]) The sad truth, however, is that some of these groups were less orthodox doctrinally than were the Roman Catholics. The sadder truth—for the successionists—is that whatever and whoever the dissenting sects were, they were not the forerunners to modern Baptists.

The popularizer of Baptist successionism in America was J. R. Graves, a man who may have had more lasting influence on Southern Baptists than any other single individual in our 125 year history. Graves died in 1893, but before his death he saw Baptist Church Succession enthroned by most Southern Baptists as unquestionable orthodoxy. It was the only "right" thing to believe! So when the Whitsitt Controversy raged during the years 1896–1899, Dr. Whitsitt often fell heir to the odious label of a "heretic." A man's view of Baptist history had become a doctrinal issue of prime importance.

You can understand the ready acceptance given to the Orchard-Graves propaganda, if you are aware of what was going on in American religious life at that time. The nineteenth century was a time of keen denominational rivalry. Most denominations in the twentieth century merely think they are God's best. But in the nineteenth century they thought they were the only ones God had. Someone recently reported seeing a billboard in front of a church which announced: "This is the only church authorized by God to represent Jesus Christ in the world." This was the prevailing notion among some denominations in the past century.

> We are the choice elected few,
> Let all the rest be damned;
> There's room enough in heaven for you,
> But we won't have heaven crammed!

That was the idea!

Public religious debates were hallmarks of the time. Great crowds would gather to hear hours of tedious theological nit-picking. Baptists vs. Methodists, Baptists vs. Church of Christ, etc. Denominational life in the nineteenth century was marked by a zealous search for authority. Religious groups were going through what psychologists might call an "identity crisis." They were trying to establish themselves, to secure some solid justification for their existence. Historians refer to this search as a "High Church" movement, and they point to the Roman Catholic Church, the Anglican Church, the Campbellites, the Lutherans, and the Baptists as evidence.

As each denomination sought to prove its claim to being the "true New Testament Church," Baptist Church Succesionism proved to be a handy bit of ammunition for Baptists. "Why," claimed the Baptists, "we began with John the Baptist, have continued in unbroken succession ever since, and we can prove it." To prove that you are the oldest is to prove that you are the "onliest"! Or so thought some Baptists in the 1800's.

II

Whitsitt challenged all this—discreetly at first. Realizing the potential explosiveness of what Whitsitt wrote, one can understand why the professor first stated his thesis in anonymous magazine articles! Date those articles 1880. Fifteen more years passed before the public knew who wrote them. In 1893 Whitsitt published a similar article in *Johnson's Universal Encyclopedia*. But this time he signed his name. The war was on!

One inflamed soul wrote a letter to the *Western Recorder*, the Kentucky Baptist state paper, and asked: "What did Dr. Whitsitt mean by writing that and publishing it in an Encyclopedia? What are the Trustees of the Seminary going to do about it? Does the *Recorder* agree with him?" The tone of the editorial response was an omen of things to come. "The Recorder," said the *Recorder*, "very emphatically does not agree with Dr. Whitsitt. We believe—past all conviction to the contrary—that the Baptists adopted immersion in the year 30, and have been immersing ever since." [4] The man who led the "loyal opposition" to Whitsitt was Dr. T. T. Eaton, editor of the Kentucky paper.

Other state papers took up the fight against Whitsitt. Associations and state conventions passed resolutions asking for Whitsitt's historical hide. He was charged with cowardice for not signing the earlier articles, with dishonesty for not finding in historical research what Baptists had always found, and with infidelity for not believing as a Baptist. And as in every controversy when men take the reins off their emotions, misinterpretation and misunderstanding resulted. Some of his opponents thought Whitsitt was saying that Baptists "invented" baptism by immersion in the seventeenth century. He never intended to say that the immersion of believers began at that time. He believed that idea came from the first century and the New Testament. He was raising a question regarding the antiquity of Baptists as a denomination and not baptism by immersion as a New Testament concept.

Friends are for tough times. Dr. Whitsitt had friends. One was Dr. John R. Sampey, a fellow faculty member of Whitsitt. At the 1896 meeting of the Baptist association in Louisville, Kentucky, Sampey "secured the floor against a bedlam of voices and talked in a passionate manner for over an hour on this issue. Boldly he defended Dr. Whitsitt's integrity, scholarly competence, and Baptist orthodoxy." [5] As a matter of fact, this Bible scholar who taught Old Testament at Southern Seminary for sixty years must have gotten rip-roaring mad because he apologized to the association the next day. The Kentucky Baptist paper described Sampey's apology as follows: "Dr. Sampey again took the floor to shake hands with the moderator and to say four things: 'I do not believe,' said he, 'I will ever inflict a speech on Long Run Association as long as that one I dumped on you yesterday. In the second place, I do not believe I will make any such wild gestures and jump over the pulpit as I did yesterday. Thirdly, Brother

Moderator, I do not believe I will ever get half as "mad" as I was yesterday. And in the fourth place, I hope, in the goodness of God, nobody will ever stir me up to get as mad as I was yesterday.' This closed the episode." [6]

The faculty at the Seminary unanimously adopted a statement in support of their president. They appealed to Southern Baptists "to stand by us, as we stand by our honored President, and to continue to give the institution your fervent prayers, your liberal support, your undiminished confidence." [7] They defended Whitsitt's scholarly competence, his scriptural soundness, and his denominational loyalty.

In spite of the faculty appeal and the tireless efforts of others to calm the waters, the situation got worse. Look at this resolution passed at the Kentucky Baptist State Convention of 1897! "Resolved, that the Trustees of the Seminary from Kentucky be requested, and they are hereby requested, to urge, insist upon and vote for the retirement of Dr. Whitsitt from the Presidency of the institution and from the Chair of Church History." [8] Four other state conventions—Mississippi, Louisiana, Arkansas, and Texas—followed the leadership of the Kentucky Convention.

More was to come. The place: Norfolk, Virginia. The date: May, 1898. The occasion: Meeting of the Southern Baptist Convention. The person: B. H. Carroll, prominent Baptist from Texas. The fly in the ointment: Carroll gave notice that he would make a motion at the 1899 meeting of the Southern Baptist Convention. The content of the motion: That the Southern Baptist Convention dissolve all relations with the Southern Baptist Theological Seminary.

The Kentucky Baptist Convention echoed B. H. Carroll

one month later. Moreover, the Kentucky convention passed another resolution denying the seminary the right "to make any report nor present any appeals of any sort whatever to this body as long as Dr. Whitsitt shall be in any manner connected with the institution." [9]

Opponents of Whitsitt had played a trump card—financial withdrawal from the seminary. The choice was painful! The seminary loses either extensive financial support while Southern Baptists lose their only seminary, or a controversial history professor who just happened also to be president loses his job. Whitsitt made the choice for the seminary and for Southern Baptist theological education. He sent a telegram to the president of the seminary Board of Trustees. It was dated July 13, 1898: "I hereby resign my office as President of the Southern Baptist Theological Seminary and Professor of Church History to take effect at the close of the session of 1898–9." One sentence, brief but to the point. The ex-president later joined the faculty of the University of Richmond in Richmond, Virginia, and taught there until 1909.

But Southern Baptist historians—the professional historians—were not through with it. They continued to teach what Whitsitt taught. Who said that times do not change? Look at this: in 1969, seventy years after Whitsitt's resignation, another church history professor at Southern Baptist Theological Seminary writes another book. He is W. Morgan Patterson and his book is *Baptist Successionism: A Critical View*. Patterson candidly says, and obviously without fear of having to resign, that the concept of Baptist church successionism rests "on precarious historical and theological foundations." [10]

III

W. O. Carver, a man who studied under Whitsitt and later became a faculty member at Southern Baptist Theological Seminary, knew Whitsitt and the Whitsitt Controversy well. In a Founder's Day address at the seminary in 1954 Carver said that the election of Whitsitt as president of the seminary in 1896 "was the occasion for the most extensive, the bitterest, and in the issue the most decisive conflict ever to disturb the Baptists of America." [11] Maybe so. But what does the Whitsitt Controversy of the 1890's have to do with Baptists of today? Are the facts of the Whitsitt issue simply a collector's item which one approaches as an antiquarian or do they touch contemporary Baptist life? They touch us.

The idea that Whitsitt was seeking to correct is very much alive to this very day. In the "Foreword" to his 1969 book, Morgan Patterson said, "The view of Baptist history examined here [successionism] is still widely held." Patterson even suspects that "it is probably the prevailing one among Baptists in the South." [12] It is a fact that you do not have to travel far in Southern Baptist life to find Baptist Church Successionism advocated. Yet the idea lacks the passionate following which it enjoyed in the nineteenth century. Southern Baptists are learning gradually that successionism is neither historically demonstrable nor theologically necessary. We cannot prove it nor do we need to do so. Valid church life is not based upon historical lineage but upon adherence to the Bible.

Another point at which this controversy touches us—have you ever heard it said that "Baptists are not Protestants"? Do you know where such a statement originated? It came from the idea that Baptists existed *before* Protestantism emerged. It is a part of the successionist approach to Baptist history. But professional Baptist historians today claim that it is an idea without historical support. Like W. H. Whitsitt before them, these historians contend that Baptists originated out of English Protestantism. W. O. Carver told of visiting Whitsitt near the end of the latter's life. Carver says that the aging historian would always ask, "How are the Baptists getting on in Kentucky?" "Then," Carver said, "he would inquire especially about the 'Protestant Baptists.' " [13] Whitsitt spearheaded a tradition in Baptist life which said, "Baptists *are* Protestants."

Maybe the most important result to come out of the Whitsitt Controversy was that it awakened Baptists in general and Southern Baptists in particular to a sense of their history. To fight over your heritage is not a good way to learn about it; but even that is better than ignoring it altogether. The Whitsitt crisis stimulated an interest in the Baptist past. Men began to look over their shoulders to see where they had come from. That is always helpful.

Not only did the Whitsitt fuss stimulate interest in the history of Baptists, Whitsitt, as Carver said, "aroused and promoted among Southern Baptists the concept and gradually and increasingly the study of their history *scientifically, objectively,* and in its wider historical context." We have often gone to history to uncover evidence which would confirm our prejudices—denominational, theological, or national. But that is the manipulation of history, not the study of history. The study of history is a moral enterprise. Moral in the sense that one must report honestly and fairly what is there. Whitsitt was trying to be guided by his intellectual honesty rather than by his denomination's bias.

He knew, however, that the scientific study of history was risky. He made an interesting entry in his diary on February 27, Thursday, 1890: "I am casting about to begin writing a work on American Baptist history. It is an herculean task, and I must keep it all to myself . . . Baptist history is a department in which 'the wise man concealeth knowledge.' It is likely I shall not be able to publish the work while I live, but I can write it out in full and make arrangements to publish it after my death, when I shall be out of reach of bigots and fools." Whether or not Whitsitt ever wrote an exhaustive survey of Baptists in America, we are not sure. But of one thing we are sure: he did not keep his knowledge of Baptist history all to himself.[14]

NOTES

1. W. Morgan Patterson, *Baptist Successionism: A Critical View* (Valley Forge, Pa.: The Judson Press, 1969) p. 28.

2. As quoted in *Ibid.* p. 25.

3. Lewis E. Rhodes, "Southern Baptists Confronting the Challenge of a Disordered Society" in *Proceedings: 1968 Christian Citizenship Seminar on Christian Action in a Disordered Society*, p. 51. Published by the Christian Life Commission of the Southern Baptist Convention.

4. These quotes appear in John R. Sampey, *Memoirs of John R. Sampey* (Nashville: Broadman Press, 1959) p. 161.

5. William A. Mueller, *A History of Southern Baptist Theological Seminary* (Nashville: Broadman Press, 1959) p. 81.

6. Sampey, *Ibid.*, p. 85.

7. As quoted in *Ibid.*, p. 164.

8. As quoted in Sampey, p. 87.

9. As quoted in Frank M. Masters, *A History of Kentucky Bap-*

tists (Middletown, Ky.: Kentucky Baptist Historical Society, 1953) p. 416.

10. Patterson, p. 6.

11. W. O. Carver, "William Heth Whitsitt: The Seminary's Martyr," (*The Review and Expositor*, October, 1954), p. 464.

12. Patterson, p. 5.

13. Carver, p. 467.

14. For a good and more extensive discussion of this controversy see James Thomas Meigs, "The Whitsitt Controversy," (*The Quarterly Review*, January, February, March, 1971) pp. 41–61.

The
"What About the Heathen?"
Controversy
or
Baptists Argue About Missions

We tend to forget. We tend to think that things have always been the way things are today. So, among other things, history is a "memory-jogger." It reminds us that the present is not the past. And often it makes us grateful that this is the case.

Baptists have not *always* been ardent advocates of missions—home or foreign. You may remember your preacher's illustration about William Carey—the father of modern missions—who stood up one day in a Baptist association in England and suggested that Baptists send missionaries to India. An older preacher barked at young Carey, "Sit down, young man. If God wants to save the heathen, He is God enough to do it without man's help." We tend to forget that.

At times Baptists have denounced missions, divided over missions, and, in some instances, destroyed missions. The speaker is missing it when he says, "Baptists have always been a great missionary people, born and bred in evangelistic fervor!" The speaker forgot his Baptist background. One wishes he were right. If he had been right, Baptists of America could have been spared one of their most damaging of all controversies—the so-called "Anti-Missions Controversy."

I

The Anti-Missions Controversy is an important chapter in Baptist life if one wants to understand contemporary attitudes of some Baptists regarding theology, worship, and support of the ministry, not to say anything concerning the missionary enterprise itself. If one ever wondered where Primitive Baptists came from or why some Baptists advocate missions but oppose mission boards, the Anti-Missions Controversy will help answer some of his questions.

In the latter part of the 1700's, the American people began a jaunt westward which carried them over the mountains and onto the frontier of Tennessee and Kentucky. A number of Baptists made that trip. Between 1790–1810 one-fourth of the Baptists of Virginia were estimated to have migrated to Kentucky. During the same period thousands of North Carolina Baptists spilled across the mountains to Tennessee. Baptists then scattered to other frontier and deep Southern regions.

Would the struggling Baptists make a go of it in their new wilderness? Absolutely! They transformed a religious jungle into a Baptist Zion. W. W. Sweet, a Methodist and one of the greatest of all American church historians, declared that no body of Christians were more suited for the frontier than were the Baptists. If you look at the figures, Sweet must have been right because Baptists experienced rapid growth beyond the mountains.

But one of our denominational ironies is just this: the frontier—an environment most conducive to the growth of Baptists—became the breeding ground and headquarters for the Anti-Missions movement among Baptists. The Anti-Missions Controversy rocked frontier Baptists from 1820 to 1840. This was prior to the organization of the Southern Baptist Convention, but the fact that Southern Baptists were without an institutional body does not mean that Baptists of the South escaped the results of the fierce missionary controversy.

Organized missionary activity among Baptists began on a nationwide scale in 1814. That was the year Luther Rice led in the formation of the Triennial Convention, a foreign missionary society that met once every three years. The thirty-three delegates who met in Philadelphia in May, 1814, had one primary purpose. They wanted to construct "a plan for eliciting, combining, and directing the energies of the whole denomination in one sacred effort, for sending the glad tidings of salvation to the heathen." The Convention appointed a Board of Foreign Missions to transact business while the Triennial Convention was not in session. (This was, I suppose, the first Executive Board!) The Board was to employ missionaries, to make sure of their qualifications, to appoint their field of labor, and to fix the amount of financial compensation. Very professional and business-like! Who could object to such a noble cause handled in such fine fashion? Baptists could! And plenty of Baptists did. The newly-formed organization became a primary target for the "anti" folk.

The Board of Foreign Missions appointed Luther Rice as "Agent." Rice travelled throughout the country rallying Baptists behind the missionary endeavor. Some he rallied. Others he angered. Few were neutral. This was one of those "for" or "against" issues—no such thing as a "silent majority" or "silent minority."

Initially, Baptists of the west responded with some enthusiasm to the idea of missions. When Luther Rice visited Kentucky in 1815, he collected more money for missions than from any other state with the exception of Massachusetts. Most of the churches in Tennessee were friendly to the foreign missions cause, also. Rice was well received in the churches there and even secured the organization of a state Foreign Mission Society.

Things changed. In Tennessee missionary societies were dissolved, and associations rescinded pro-missions resolutions. Speaking of the anti-missionary sentiment, one contemporary said, "The current of prejudice had gradually swollen, until now no one cares to resist it."

Anti-missionism spread rapidly and extensively. Not a man ventured "to open his mouth in favor of any benevolent enterprise or action. The missionary societies were dissolved, and the associations rescinded all their resolutions by which they were in any way connected with these measures." [1]

Within one decade, 1820–1830, the anti-mission movement threw Kentucky Baptists in chaos. Anti-mission forces in Mississippi destroyed the first state-wide Baptist organization and nearly demolished the second, founded in 1836. Even in the Old Dominion of Virginia, twelve of thirty-four associations in 1845 were aggressively anti-mission. Look at the decline of missionary interest in Ohio! In 1820 Baptist churches of that region contributed $547.09 to missions, from 1821–1828 they gave zero, and in 1829 and 1830 the gifts were $10 and $5 respectively. Baptists of Alabama,

Georgia, Missouri, Illinois, Indiana, and Louisiana were also affected. By 1846 there were 68,068 anti-mission Baptists in the United States. 45,000 of these were located in the frontier states.

II

What happened? Why the change of attitude regarding missions? It is an interesting story, and while the whole cannot be told here, enough can be said to identify the major forces at work in this crucial period of American Baptist history.

One of the major factors in the rise of anti-missionism was jealousy—*unredeemed ministerial jealousy!* The frontier Baptist preachers were generally uneducated, often downright illiterate. In 1817 the Triennial Convention began sending "home" missionaries to the frontier. John Mason Peck was the most famous of these missionaries. These preachers from the East were a more educated breed. While the typical frontier preacher was a farmer during the week and a preacher on Sundays, receiving his education mostly between the handles of a plow, the missionary preachers from the "urban East" had what the frontiersmen called "book larnin'." This threatened the grubby backwoodsmen.

One frontier preacher whose personal jealousy had transformed itself into antagonism toward organized missions is reported to have said: "We don't care anything about them missionaries that's gone amongst them heathens way off yonder." When pressed for reasons for his hostility, he admitted, "Well, if you must know, . . . you know the big trees in the woods overshadow the little ones; and these missionaries will be all great, learned men, and the people will all go to hear them preach, and we shall all be put down. That's the objection." [2] At least he was honest! But there are some things in life that are tragic, even when we are honest about them. Jealousy is one of them!

From this jealousy of educated missionaries grew a suspicion of ministerial education in general. Baptists had not always scorned education. To the contrary, Baptists in Colonial America had put a high value on an educated clergy. Neither did all Baptists on the frontier view lightly the importance of an enlightened clergy. But amidst the deprivation and grubby individualism of the frontier, education was not considered a paramount factor in the life of a minister.

The primary issue was whether the preacher had received a call from God to the ministry. One anti-missionary association in Alabama summarized the frontiersman point of view: "As to the education we know no objection, provided it is received *before* a call to the ministry, for Paul says, 'Let every man abide in the same calling wherein he was called' . . . Oh, what an insult to Deity, that men should say that God has no power to qualify men for the ministry, after He has called them." An anti-missionary preacher compared "theological schools to make preachers" to "the bottomless pit spoken of in Revelations. For a bottomless pit has no foundation in the Scriptures as an institution of God."

"Highfalutin" language from the pulpit was not impressive. But a perspiring face, a passionate voice, and homespun illustrations were impressive. One said that when pioneer preachers stood to preach "they usually threw the reins upon the neck of feeling and let her run full speed." [3] With their emphasis altogether on "heart" rather than "head" one can understand their fear of the educated brethren from the East. But it is altogether possible that some of the harsh feelings were elicited by the eastern preachers who paraded their learning.

Closely related to the ministerial jealousy between uneducated and educated was a sectional jealousy between East and West. Westerners saw Easterners as blue-blooded aristocrats. Easterners viewed Westerners as uncouth backwoodsmen. Compounding this geographical rivalry for Baptists was the fact that mission societies originated in the East; they demanded a membership fee that was sometimes a considerable fee; they were controlled in the East. Given their previously established prejudices toward the East, frontiersmen saw the missionary movement as an obvious nefarious plot whereby they were to be bilked for the benefit of money-mad city-slickers. The pioneers bowed up at the smell of what John Taylor called "the New England Rat."

A second factor which aided the rise of anti-missionism was suspicion of missionary organizations. Frontier Baptists interpreted the increasing number of missionary societies as a trend toward Centralization in church government and authority. Fearing that the independence of the local churches would be swallowed up in an eastern ecclesiastical superstructure, many churches and preachers lashed out at the missionary societies.

In his anti-mission pamphlet Daniel Parker noted that God did not send Jonah to Nineveh through a missionary society, nor was he "sent to a seminary of learning to prepare him to preach to these Gentiles; but was under the tuition of a special order of God, and was in no case under the direction of any body of men whatever, neither did he look back to a society formed to raise money for his support." The only organization the Bible knew was the church of Christ!

Baptists had always been rather protective of the freedom and authority of local church autonomy. The individualism of frontier living compounded this trend. When someone therefore began talking about a missionary society which had *authority* to send missionaries wherever it desired, many Baptists began to wonder if a conspiracy was at work against the local churches.

There was a third factor which spurred on anti-missionism: money! The foreign missionaries like Judson, the travelling agents like Luther Rice, the home missionaries like Peck, and the missionary societies like the Triennial Convention wanted money! This sounded strange to a group who didn't pay their own preachers. And frontier Baptists never became infatuated with that habit. As a matter of fact, many of the frontier preachers would have never thought of asking for money for themselves. Some frontier ministers thought it was unethical to receive pay for doing the Lord's work. God's gospel should be dispensed free of charge! One person said of the frontiersmen that they "loved the gospel, and they loved its ministers, but the sound of money drove all the good feelings from their heart." [4] A Baptist preacher contended that the Baptist doctrine concerning the ministry was: "The Lord keep thee humble, and we'll keep thee poor." [5]

Luther Rice visited the Elkhorn Baptist Association in Kentucky in 1815. Trying to fire the missionary imagination of the Kentucky Baptists, he was also seeking to secure their monetary support. One of the men who was later to become a leader in the Anti-Missions movement was "turned off" by Rice's appeal for money. He described Luther Rice's sermon with biting sarcasm: "When Luther rose up, the assembly of thousands, seemed strickened with his appearance. A tall, pale looking well-dressed young man, with all the solemn appearance of one who was engaged in the work of the Lord, and perhaps he thought he was. He spoke some handsome things about the kingdom of Christ; but every stroke he gave seemed to men MONEY. He had the more pathos the nearer he came getting the money." [6] For this anti-missionist the entire missionary endeavor of the Triennial Convention was based upon the evil principles of "money and power."

Suspicion breeds distortion. Anti-missionists circulated stories saying that "if the people went to hear a missionary they would be taxed and would be compelled to pay twenty-five cents for every sermon they heard, and every one baptized, there would be a tax of fifty cents to pay, and every year a tax of one dollar." A classic case of misrepresentation growing out of the failure of conflicting parties to communicate!

Everything has to have a theology. There is a theology of sex. A theology of violence. A theology of ecology, and on and on and on. There was also a theology of anti-missions. Which comes first: theology or practice? Do we do a thing and then theologize it, or do we think a thing and then practice it?

It is often impossible to tell. My guess is that in the case of the anti-missions controversy, theology probably came in second—to justify practice. At any rate, theology was also an important ingredient in the recipe for anti-missionism.

The theology of the anti-missions controversy was hyper-Calvinism—that old idea that a sovereign God does not need the help of finite man to bring in the Kingdom of Heaven. Baptists viewed as gross heresy anything that smacked of the Methodist concept of salvation by works. "Election" and "predestination" were the "in" words of a person opposed to missions. "Converting the heathen is God's work," he would cry: "Let God do it!"

One association in Mississippi, denouncing the missionary program, clearly demonstrated the prevailing theology of the anti-missions movement: "Surely you must have a great thirst for money that you should beg it in the name of converting the heathen!—for if you know anything about God, you know this, that it is His prerogative to convert the heathen, or as many of them as he wants converted." And so were born the Primitive Baptists!

Daniel Parker, father of a group of Baptists with the intriguing name of the Two-Seed-in-the-Spirit Predestinarian Baptists, represented the most extreme example of hyper-Calvinism. His theology was simple and understandably anti-missionary. He said there were two seeds present in the life stream of humanity, one good and the other evil. Every person is born with one seed or the other, and nothing can be done about it. Children born of the divine seed are children of God; children born of the evil seed are children of the devil. Missions are superfluous, for man cannot change what is already fixed and predestined. Parker's Two-Seed group still exists—barely. In 1945 they had 16 churches with a total membership of 201. But one would hardly expect great growth from that kind of thinking.

Bad theology is a big obstacle. Needed change is often crippled by wrong thinking. The missionary movement was retarded and, in some areas, buried because of bad theology.

To summarize: here are four of the major factors in the rise of the Anti-Missions Controversy—one, the personal factor of ministerial jealousy; two, the organizational factor of fear of centralization; three, the financial factor of ministerial support; four, the theological factor of hyper-Calvinism.

But there was a fifth thing, without which the others would have been impotent—the personnel of the Anti-Missions Controversy. A trio it was: John Taylor, Alexander Campbell, and Daniel Parker. All were implacable and persuasive foes of Baptist missions. It just so happened that they were also three of the most influential preachers on the frontier.

John Taylor fired the first significant shot. In 1819 he unleashed a furious polemic with the bland title of *Thoughts on Missions*. But only the title was bland. For it was Taylor who referred to the missionary efforts as the "New England rat." It was Taylor who said that the missionaries love money like a horse-leech loves blood. And it was Taylor who dubbed Luther Rice "a modern Tetzel." (Tetzel, you may recall, was the Catholic priest who angered Martin Luther by selling indulgences.) With age Taylor mellowed, and by the time of his death he was living at peace with his missionary brethren. The old warhorse repented of his rampage, but not before inflicting untold harm on the organized missionary effort.

Daniel Parker died unrepentant. Neither age nor argument could tame his spirit. To his disciples, he was a Moses, a leader without peer. To missionary Baptists, he was "the notorious Daniel Parker." On one occasion Parker was at an associational meeting where Luther Rice preached and collected an offering for missions. Someone asked Elder Parker if he made a contribution. He answered "No!" and that "He had no counterfeit half dollars; if he had he would have thrown in, but as he had none he would not throw away good money for such an object."

John Mason Peck described Parker as "one of those singular and extraordinary beings whom Divine Providence permits to arise as a scourge to his church." To be sure, Peck played ball for the opposite team, but it is without question that Parker was born in the objective mood. His life, sermons, and writings reeked with negativism. He found his security in being against something. With intemperate zeal, he lashed out at the missions movement.

The last of the three fighters was Alexander Campbell, a man whose name is most commonly identified with the body of Christians known as the Disciples of Christ or the Churches of Christ. But Campbell was a Baptist for a while. In fact, long enough to build up a massive following and lead thousands of Baptists out of the denomination.

The Baptists and the Campbellites divided because of several differences, including their understanding of baptism; but one of the basic problems was Campbell's attitude toward missionary organizations—unscriptural societies, as he called them. Like John Taylor, he later changed his mind on the question of missionary societies. But this was after he had helped divide Baptists over the issue.

When the smoke had cleared from the Anti-Missions Controversy, Baptist ranks in the South were thinner. And yet here may be an example of the oft-stated idea that quantitative decline does not mean a qualitative set-back. Pro-missionary Baptists came out of this abrasive conflict more committed than ever before to the idea of Christian missions.

And though they would engage in later arguments concerning the method of missions—whether through boards or local churches—most Southern Baptists came out of the anti-missions crisis firmly committed to some form of centralized missionary operations. At the same time that Southern Baptists organized their Convention in 1845, they also established Foreign and Home Mission Boards.

The Anti-Missions Controversy also helped chart the theological course for future Southern Baptists. At least it ruled out one option: hyper-Calvinism. Missionary Baptists of the South continued to affirm the sovereignty of God in human history, but they refused to hide behind that idea when it undercut human responsibility. Southern Baptists came out of the missionary melee believing that man is more than puppet.

NOTES

1. As quoted in A. H. Newman, *A History of the Baptist Churches in the United States* (New York: The Christian Literature Company, 1894) p. 437, 438.

2. As quoted in T. Scott Miyakawa, *Protestants and Pioneers* (Chicago: The University of Chicago Press, 1964) p. 148.

3. As quoted in Walter Browlow Posey, *The Baptist Church in the Lower Mississippi Valley, 1776–1845* (University of Kentucky: The University of Kentucky Press, 1957) p. 25.

4. *Ibid.*, p. 32.

5. As quoted in *Ibid.*, p. 32.

6. As quoted in Robert A. Baker, *A Baptist Source Book* (Nashville: Broadman Press, 1966) p. 80.

The "What About the Blacks?" Controversy
or
Baptists Argue Over Slavery and Segregation

One would have to be a religious Rip Van Winkle to be unaware of the fact that Southern Baptists, among other American churchmen, have been going through a revolution as of late. And when all the rhetoric is silenced, one of the major reasons for all the fuss is the question, "What about the blacks?" The fuss is not a new one for Southern Baptists, however. Nor has it been subdued.

Davis C. Woolley, the late Executive Secretary of the Historical Commission of the Southern Baptist Convention, wrote that the racial issue "is one of the most inflammatory subjects ever to be discussed in the Convention." [1] After scanning Southern Baptist history, one may think that Woolley grossly understated the case. It has not only been inflammatory; it has been explosive!

I

Like the English Baptists of the seventeenth century, the

Southern Baptist Convention was born in the fire of controversy. What caused the fire? Was it theological in nature? Did Southern Baptists create their own Convention because they feared theological liberalism among Baptists in the North? No, not really. When the delegates to the first Southern Baptist Convention gathered in Augusta, Georgia, in May, 1845, they were not protesting doctrinal heresy. Said those first Southern Baptists from Augusta, "Let not the extent of this disunion be exaggerated . . . Northern and Southern Baptists are still brethren. *They differ in no article of the faith.* They are guided by the same principles of gospel order . . . We do not regard the rupture as extending to foundation principles, nor can we think that the great body of our Northern brethren will so regard it." [2] Theology was not the issue in Augusta. Not at all!

Nor was ecclesiology (the doctrine of the church) the primary issue at Augusta. One interpretation of the organization of the Southern Baptist Convention is that Baptists of the South wanted one type of denominational structure while those of the North wanted another. But this idea has probably been given too much attention.

It is a fact that when Baptists of America formed their first national organization (the Triennial Convention) in 1814, there were differences of opinion regarding what type of organizational structure would be best. Some wanted a very decentralized approach to denominational life. Others wanted a more centralized approach. The centralized approach was more popular in the South. Decentralization eventually won out. Individual societies (such as Foreign Missions Society, Home Missions Society, etc.) were organized, rather than *one* denominational Convention.

But when Southern Baptists met in 1845 to form a Southern Baptist organization, they constructed a more centralized denomination than Baptists in America had at that time. Some Southern leaders wanted the centralized approach all along. Now they had their opportunity. They would do it "their way."

One must insist, however, that the nature of the denominational organization was neither the occasion nor the underlying cause of the formation of the Southern Baptist Convention. And one only has to read what Southern Baptists themselves said at their first meeting to know that this is true. Baptists in America would probably have never suffered denominational division over ecclesiology. It simply had not been that hot an issue among them. In Augusta ecclesiology was not the issue at stake.

There is a third issue, beyond theology and ecclesiology, which possibly would have created organizational division among Baptists in America. But it was certainly not a major cause or immediate factor in the formation of the Southern Convention. This was the issue of home missions.

Baptists in America formed the American Baptist Home Missionary Society in 1832. Shortly after its formation, Baptists of the deep South, the Southwest, and the West began to air objections. They felt that a disproportionate number of missionaries were sent into Northern and Eastern regions, to the sad neglect of their own territories. The Society, however, was not engaged in a deliberate policy to overlook the needs of these areas.[3]

Nonetheless, calls went out prior to 1845 for the organization of a new Society which would better attend to the needs of the West, Southwest, and South. None of these calls bore permanent fruit. It is altogether possible, however, that this issue would have eventually separated Baptists in America. Had it done so, the Baptist division might have been more East-West than North-South. But home missions was not the primary concern of the brethren who travelled to Augusta.

Well, let me finally answer the question. What was the issue, the major issue, and the immediate issue in the organization of the Southern Baptist Convention? It was *slavery*, the same issue which tore the innards out of the nation a few years later. A cultural earthquake struck this young nation during the years 1830–1865. But before the quake created a political chasm between North and South, it had sliced the churches down their Mason-Dixon Line.

The Southern Baptist Convention was organized in defense of the mid-nineteenth century Southern culture. But lest you quickly and self-righteously blast the Baptists of 125 years ago and threaten to leave Southern Baptists to join a denomination unmarred by the scar of slavery, I must add another word. Baptists were not alone. The octopus of culture has little respect for denominational boundaries. It will choke the Christian ideals of a Presbyterian or a Methodist just as soon as it will a Baptist. Evidence: Methodists of the South formed their slavery-justifying denomination a few days before the Baptists; Presbyterians followed a few years later.

Churchmen of the South had not always been unanimous in their justification of slavery, just as churchmen of the North had not been unanimous in their condemnation of it. Baptists, North and South, denounced slavery in the 1700's and early 1800's. In 1790 some Virginia Baptists affirmed "that slavery is a violent deprivation of the rights of nature and inconsistent with a republic government." They suggested that Baptists "make use of every legal measure to extirpate the horrid evil from the land."

In 1796 the Ketocton Association of Virginia declared that slavery was a transgression of the Divine Law. The Association also appointed a committee to draw up a suggested plan of general emancipation. Other associations in other states passed anti-slavery resolutions.

But the Baptist voice against slavery was not loud. Nor was it widespread. Nor was it long in meeting stiff opposition. The Ketocton Association's plan of emancipation is indicative of the situation. According to a Virginia Baptist historian the association was "treading upon delicate ground." He went on to say that the emancipation plan "excited considerable tumult in the churches, and accordingly in their letters to the next association they remonstrated so decidedly that the Association resolved to take no further steps in the business." [4]

As Baptist associations and committees encountered grass root hostility, they backed off. They then began to say that slavery was an economic and civil issue and did not therefore properly belong in religious discussions. This rationale for evading the plight of the black man would long be a strategy in Baptist circles of the South.

From about 1790, Southern Baptists' attitudes regarding slavery stiffened. More and more, Baptists, with other Southerners, justified and defended slavery. What caused this stiffening on the part of the Southerners?

For one thing, a revolution in Southern agriculture occurred. Whitney's cotton gin in 1792, plus other developments, made slavery more economically profitable. Slavery suffered less denunciation as cotton became king. Also, the growing spirit of Northern abolitionism played a role. A powerful sentiment for emancipation emerged in the North in the 1830's. Abolitionists eventually attacked more than the system of slavery; they scorned slaveholders too. Sectional polarization developed in a hurry. Southerners became defensive not only of their Christian character. They also defended slavery. And often they did it in the name of the gospel. Northerners became aggressive in the name of the same gospel.

II

As stated previously, the first national organization of Baptists was the Triennial Convention. Organized in 1814, its primary focus was foreign missions. By 1832 Baptists of America had formed a Home Missions Society. These two organizations became the focal point of the slave controversy for Baptists, North and South.

The Triennial Convention was experiencing agitation and division over the slavery issue as early as 1834. By 1840 militant Baptist abolitionists in the North had organized themselves into a Baptist Anti-Slavery Convention. They advocated immediate emancipation. They also became letter writers. In a letter to their Northern Baptist brethren, who were more moderate on slavery, the abolitionists argued that all Northern Baptists were obligated to take action against Southern Baptists if slavery persisted. And in a letter to Southern Baptists, "Southern churches were urged to confess the sinfulness of holding slaves, to remonstrate against civil laws which entrenched the system, and if these plans were disregarded, to gather their families and possessions and emigrate to the North." [5] Baptists of the South were not tickled with the contents of that letter.

The issue was surfacing—should slaveholders be allowed fellowship in the Triennial Convention? And more specifically, should a slaveholder be appointed a missionary by the Convention? Times of tension often present moderates with the leadership. Such was the case here—for a few years. The moderates of the North and the pro-slavery Southerners joined forces to guarantee the peace and future of the Triennial Convention.

This uneasy alliance could prop up the Convention only for a while. After three or four years, the Triennial Convention, like Humpty Dumpty, would have a great fall. (And as it turned out, all the Baptists in the United States have not been able to put the Convention back together again.) But before the collapse, moderate Northerners and pro-slavery Southerners got the Triennial Convention to take a position of "neutrality" on the slave issue.

At the 1844 meeting in Philadelphia, the Triennial Convention reaffirmed a position of neutrality. This was a position taken several times before, and it was based upon the fact that the Triennial Convention had only one purpose: foreign missions. Members of the Convention could speak as individuals on the slave question, but no one could speak *in* the Convention or *for* the Convention on this divisive issue.

Harmony within the Convention took priority over stand-taking on slavery. Southerners thought they had the victory. But constant and forceful pressure was exerted on the Northern Baptists to disassociate themselves from the evil of slavery. Neutrality was impossible forever. During the Protestant Reformation, burly and impulsive Martin Luther once said of Erasmus, his cautious humanist friend, "He wants to walk on eggs without breaking them." The Triennial Convention tried that for awhile. But a showdown was inevitable.

Baptists of Alabama were not convinced that the Triennial Convention was really neutral on the issue. And they had reason for suspicion.[6] So on November 25, 1844, Baptists of that state addressed a fateful letter to the Board of Managers of the Triennial Convention. Consisting of a Preamble and six Resolutions, the letter called for candor from the Northern brethren. The essence of the letter is found in the second resolution. It is important enough to quote in full:

Resolved, that our duty requires us, at this crisis, to demand from the proper authorities in all those bodies to whose funds we have contributed, or with whom we have in any way been connected, the distinct, explicit avowal that slaveholders are eligible, and entitled, equally with non-slaveholders, to all the privileges and immunities of their several unions; and especially to receive any agency mission, or other appointment, which may fall in the scope of their operations or duties.

School was out! It was a time for candor. The Board of the Triennial Convention issued a stinging reply. "If . . . any one should offer himself as a missionary, having slaves, and should insist on retaining them as his property," they said, "we could not appoint him." That was candor! But just to be sure to avoid ambiguity they went on. "One thing is certain; we can never be a party to any arrangement which would imply approbation of slavery."

Alabama Baptists had also threatened to withdraw financial support. The paraphrased response of the Northerners could be stated as "Take your money and blow." Southern

Baptists could take a hint. They blew—to Augusta.

Virginia Baptists considered the action of the Board of the Triennial Convention "an outrage" on Southern rights. They argued that the Board had pulled off an unlawful and unconstitutional act. Technically, that was true. For the Constitution of the Triennial Convention, framed by slaveholders and non-slaveholders alike, did not address itself to slavery. Moreover, the 1844 Triennial Convention had approved a resolution which chased the slave issue out of the Convention with a declaration of "neutrality."

The Board's anti-slavery statement was dubbed "a flagrant breach of trust." The Virginia Baptist Foreign Mission Society said, "To remain united with the Board is impossible. Self-respect forbids it." Subsequently, they adopted and circulated the following resolution which resulted in the organization of the Southern Baptist convention:

Resolved . . . that in the present exigency, it is important that those brethren who are aggrieved by the recent decision of the Board in Boston, should hold a Convention, to confer on the best means of promoting the Foreign Mission cause, and other interests of the Baptist denomination in the South.

Augusta, Georgia was suggested as the place for the Convention and May 8, 1845 the date. Southern Baptists heeded both suggestions.

A few voices among Southern Baptists discouraged the idea of a new Convention. For example, the Tennessee Baptist Foreign Mission Society, while believing the board of the Triennial Convention had violated a trust and "rendered themselves justly obnoxious to the censure of the whole church," nevertheless advised against the proposed new

Convention. The Tennessee Society believed the Triennial Convention, in its next general meeting, would have reversed the decision of the Board. But Baptists of the South did not plan to wait two years to find out.

Two hundred ninety-three "delegates," representing such diverse Baptist bodies as local churches, ministers' conferences, associations, state conventions, educational institutions, and missionary societies, met in Augusta and voted to organize a new Convention. They indicated that the division was "painful" but necessary because "our brethren have pressed upon every inch of our privileges and our sacred rights."

The purpose of the Convention, according to Article II of the Constitution, was "to promote Foreign and Domestic Missions, and other important objects connected with the Redeemer's kingdom." In the public statement which Southern Baptists sent out there is a paragraph which depicts not only the purpose of the Convention but also their basic rationale toward slavery.

Our objects, then, are the extension of the Messiah's kingdom, and the glory of God. Not disunion with any of his people; not the upholding of any form of human policy or civil rights; but God's glory, and Messiah's increasing reign; in the promotion of which, we find no necessity for relinquishing any of our civil rights. We will never interfere with *what is Caesar's*. We will not compromit what is God's.[7]

What was the "what is Caesar's" which was placed in italics? Slavery, obviously. The pattern established by early Baptist associations and continued awhile by the Triennial Convention, of dodging the slave issue by declaring it beyond the religious domain, persisted.

III

Augusta didn't settle things. Southern Baptists were not finished with the question, "What about the blacks?"

From slavery, Southern Baptists eventually turned to debate racial prejudice and its social manifestation— segregation. This time the disagreement would not involve Northern and Southern Baptists. This time Southern Baptists argued among themselves. There would be no organizational division, but fiery debate would abound.

The year 1954 was a pivotal one for race relations in America. In that year the Supreme Court of the United States issued its landmark decision on public school segregation. And in their annual convention of the same year, the Southern Baptist Convention adopted a report of their Christian Life Commission which acknowledged that the Court decision "is in harmony with the constitutional guarantee of equal freedom to all citizens, and with the Christian principles of equal justice and love for all men." The adopted report also commended the Supreme Court for deferring the application of school desegregation, urged Baptists to conduct themselves in the spirit of Christ in the period of adjustment, affirmed a belief in the public school system of America, and advised Christian statesmen and leaders to use their leadership positions to avert new and bitter prejudices.

Southern Baptists had spoken as a Convention to the issue of race relations before 1954. One may find resolutions and recommendations regarding race in the Convention proceedings of 1939, 1940, and 1941. According to T. B. Maston (the man who, more than any other, has scrutinized the subject of Southern Baptists and race relations), Southern Baptists took their most significant convention action in 1947. That year messengers to the Convention adopted a special report which said many good things such as, "We shall think of the Negro as a person and treat him accordingly;" "We shall continually strive as individuals to conquer all prejudice"; "We shall teach our children that prejudice is un-Christian," etc.[8]

Individual Southern Baptists had also spoken out on the race issue. While Hitler and his crusade of anti-Semitism hovered over Europe and the world of 1942, one Baptist editor wrote, "Until we break down racial prejudices within the boundaries of our own land and prove by its working that a program of racial adjustment is practical, we shall be heard with little serious attention when we speak about removing the larger and far more complicated racial antipathies and antagonism which the would-be dictators of the world are using today for their own advancements." [9]

Notice two things about Southern Baptists and race prior to 1954. One, most of their public pronouncements came through Convention resolutions. It has always been much easier to adopt a resolution in a convention than to implement it in a local church. Every pastor knows that. And secondly, the resolutions which Baptists were adopting had to do with racial prejudice in a general sense. Few addressed themselves to the question of integration.

Following the Supreme Court decision of 1954 the racial situation in the South became most intense. The emerging Civil Rights Resolution angered many Southern whites—many of whom were Baptist. Desegregation came gradually. When Baptist students at Ridgecrest Assembly requested in 1946 that Negro Baptist students be represented at the next annual encampment, the petition was first refused. The policy of segregation at Baptist assemblies was later changed. Southern Baptist seminaries did not officially desegregate until 1951, while Wayland Baptist College in Texas became the first white Baptist college in the South to enroll a Negro in the same year. Today nearly all Baptist institutions are integrated.

Integrating denominational institutions was much easier than integrating local churches. In 1968 the Home Mission Board of the Convention conducted a study which indicated 510 churches had black members. 3,724 other churches expressed a willingness to receive Negro members. Both of those figures have increased since 1968.

Desegregation has come gradually, painfully, and certainly not without controversy among Southern Baptists. Churches were divided, pastors dismissed, and editors rebuked. As recently as 1968 the Southern Baptist Convention, meeting in Houston, Texas, engaged in a spirited controversy over the adoption of a document called "A Statement Concerning the Crisis in Our Nation." Among many other things, the statement said, "We will personally accept every Christian as a brother bel ved in the Lord and welcome to the fellowship of faith and worship every person irrespective of race or class." [10] Before the statement was adopted by a vote of 5,687 (72.85%) to 2,119 (27.15%), an attempt had been made to table the main motion. Once again, however, this was a public statement made by a convention. Action was left to individuals and local churches.

According to volume III of the *Encyclopedia of Southern Baptists*, in 1971 there were at least four predominantly white congregations in the Southern Baptist Convention who had Negro pastors. To be sure, a very small number. But that is a long, long way from May, 1845 in Augusta, Georgia. Some Southern Baptists might agree today with the words of T. B. Maston, written in 1967, "Progress has been made and is being made, but when we compare what we have done with what we should have done it seems mighty little." [11] It is an old, nagging, controversial question for Southern Baptists, and it keeps coming up: "What about the Blacks?"

NOTES

1. Davis C. Woolley, "Major Convention Crises Over a Century and a Quarter," (*Review and Expositor*, Spring, 1970) p. 80.
2. *Proceedings of the Southern Baptist Convention, 1845*, p. 17. Italics mine for emphasis.
3. See Robert A. Baker, *Relations Between Northern and Southern Baptists*, (Published by the author, Fort Worth, Texas, 1948), pp. 27–39.
4. Robert B. Semple, *A History of the Rise and Progress of the Baptists in Virginia* revised by G. W. Beale, (Richmond, Va., Pitt and Dickinson, 1894) p. 392.
5. Baker, *Relations Between Northern and Southern Baptists*, p. 50.
6. The Home Mission Society had recently refused to appoint a slaveholder as a missionary. The slaveholder had been suggested by Georgia Baptists, but Georgia Baptists also made it clear that this was a "test case." The candidate was turned down, so the Mission Society said, not because he was a slaveholder, but because he represented a "test case." Southerners were enraged. It was this event which aroused Alabama Baptists to write the Board of Managers of the Triennial Convention.
7. Most of the documents pertaining to the formation of the Southern Baptist Convention may be seen in the following three

sources: *Proceedings of the Southern Baptist Convention, 1845;* Robert A. Baker, *A Baptist Source Book with Particular Reference to Southern Baptists,* (Nashville, Tenn., Broadman Press, 1966); *The Quarterly Review,* vol. 30, numbers 1 and 2.

8. *Southern Baptist Convention Annual,* 1947, pp. 47–48.

9. As quoted in Kenneth K. Bailey, "Southern Baptists, 1940–1963" (*Baptist History and Heritage,* January, 1968) p. 20.

10. *Southern Baptists Convention Annual,* 1968, p. 68.

11. T. B. Maston, "Southern Baptists and the Negro," (*The Baptist Student,* May, 1967) p. 28.

The "What About Other Denominations?" Controversy
or
Baptists Argue About the Church

The following incidents are true. I know; they happened to me! Names have been deleted, not in order to protect the innocent, but because I can't remember all the names. The incidents come out of twelve years of pastoral experience in Baptist churches.

Incident One. While a seminary student at New Orleans, I became pastor of a rural church in southeast Louisiana. About two weeks after I went to the church a lady of the community, whom I thought was a member of the church, came to my house wanting to talk. Here was her problem: She and her husband had recently moved into the community after living most of their lives in Chicago, San Diego, Brooklyn, and other such "foreign" regions. Both the Mr. and the Mrs. were Baptists. But, they were American Baptists (Northern) and not Southern Baptists. She had been reluctant to join the rural church in southeast Louisiana because she had heard that she might have to be re-baptized. Her question: "Do Southern Baptists not accept baptism from Baptist churches of other Conventions? That's what I've heard." My answer: "There is some truth to what you heard. A few Southern Baptists might have reservations about your baptism."

Incident Two. After a worship service one night a young ex-Quaker-lady-recently-turned-Baptist walked up to me and said, "They told me the other night in Training Union that Baptists aren't Protestants; where in the world did they get such an idea?" I can't tell you all that I told her, but a part of the answer is found in chapter II of this book, and a little more of the answer is found in this chapter.

Incident Three. I was speaking at a Presbyterian youth retreat on the subject, "Who are the Baptists?" After I had worked hard for twenty minutes painting Baptists as a loving, tolerant, open group of twentieth-century Christians, a teenager blurted out, "Why won't you Baptists let us Presbyterians take the Lord's Supper with you?" I explained that some Baptists would welcome her to the Lord's Table. I did not, however, bother to explain why some Baptists would frown on "open communion." That is part of what this chapter is about.

Incident Four. "Is it true," asked a Methodist man, "that Southern Baptists won't accept my baptism even though I was immersed as an adult?"

Incident Five. "Why is it," asked an Episcopalian collegian, "that Southern Baptists don't participate in more inter-denominational activities? Do you folks think you are the only true church?"

End of incidents.

But *why* have some Baptists demanded other Baptists to

be rebaptized? *Where* did Southern Baptists get the notion that Baptists aren't Protestants? *Why* have some Baptists made "a thing" out of limiting the Lord's Supper to Baptists? *Why* do most Baptist churches reject "alien immersion" —immersion performed by other denominations? And *why* have Baptists been shy about inter-denominational activities?

Well, as in most cases, the answer is complex. Many factors and ideas shape denominational life. But if one understands a movement known as Landmarkism, he can better interpret the above incidents.

I

Landmarkism is a movement which developed among Baptists in America in the 1850's and whose influence is still felt to this very day. A basic idea of Landmarkism is "the sole validity of Baptist churches." [1] In other words, *Baptist churches are the only real Christian churches!* Church historians refer to such a movement as "high churchism"; sociologists would dub it "exclusivistic"; and ordinary churchmen, reared in the twentieth century, would probably write it off as "denominational arrogance." Call it what you will, it is one of the facts of Baptist history.

The Landmark movement exerted some influence on Baptists of the North. Its greatest foothold, however, was among Southern Baptists. And while the excessively rigid attitude of the movement is dead or dying (few, if any, Southern Baptists maintain today that Baptist churches are the *only* true churches), vestiges of Landmarkism continue to crop up in Southern Baptist life.

There were three primary leaders in the rise of Landmarkism. They have often been spoken of as "The Great Triumvirate." The father and popularizer of the movement was J. R. Graves (1820–1893). Originally from Vermont, Graves finally settled in Nashville, Tennessee, in 1845, about two months after the formation of the Southern Baptist Convention. He became a member of the First Baptist Church in Nashville, where he eventually was embroiled in a controversy with the pastor, R. B. C. Howell. In 1846 Graves became assistant editor and in 1848 editor of *Tennessee Baptist.* He held that post until his death in 1893.

He was a pastor, evangelist, editor, author, publisher, denominational leader; he was many things, but most of all he was a controversalist! Possessed with an overdose of charisma and locomotive energy, he drove himself tirelessly. As his son-in-law and biographer said, "There was no still life in him. He had no idea of resting like the lark in the soft dawn of morning." [2]

J. R. Graves was a Baptist come to do battle. His first sermon, preached in Jessamine County, Kentucky, was an omen. His text was, "Adam, where art thou?" and in it he gutted the religious chameleons, those void of fixed religious principles, those too timid to announce and defend their faith. He was not the kind to compromise when he was convinced, and he was never unconvinced. "When he unsheathed his sword he threw the scabbard away," said his admiring son-in-law, but many of his fiercest opponents would have quickly agreed with that assessment. After reading him—and reading about him—he is the kind of guy you wish you could have known personally, so that your love could be more legitimate or your disapproval more passionate.

Through his efforts and influence, Graves spread Land-markism rapidly and extensively among Baptists in the South and Southwest. The author of the article on J. R. Graves in the *Encyclopedia of Southern Baptists* said, "He influenced Southern Baptist life of the nineteenth century in more ways, and probably to a greater degree, than any other person." Many Southern Baptist historians agree.

Dr. J. M. Pendleton was the second most important person-ality in the Landmark movement. A pastor and professor, Pendleton was the theologian of Landmarkism. In 1852 Pen-dleton, pastor of the Baptist church in Bowling Green, Ken-tucky, invited J. R. Graves to preach a revival meeting in the church. After Graves arrived in Bowling Green and discov-ered that Pendleton was in the habit of receiving "alien immersion" as valid baptism, he almost returned to Nash-ville. Pendleton prevailed upon him to stay.

During the revival the evangelist must have come down hard on the issue of baptism—denouncing both "alien im-mersion" and infant baptism—because "there was considera-ble excitement among Pedobaptists (infant-baptizers) on the subject of baptism and several sermons were afterward preached by Methodist and Presbyterian ministers." [3] Seven-ty-five people were converted in that revival. And while the pastor was not numbered among those seventy-five, he had been converted—to J. R. Graves' thinking. The paragraph below, taken from Pendleton's autobiography, reflects not only the growing relationship between the two men, but also the origin of the term "Landmark."

From the time of the meeting . . . , I became a regular contributor to the *Tennessee Baptist*, a weekly sheet published in Nashville,

J. R. Graves, editor. I wrote on various subjects and was requested to write several articles on this question: "Ought Baptists To Recognize Pedobaptist Preachers as Gospel Ministers?" I answered in the negative, and wrote four articles which were afterward published in pamphlet form under the title, "An Old Landmark Re-set." Bro. Graves furnished the title, for he said the "Old Landmark once stood, but had fallen, and needed to be "re-set." So much for the name.[4]

This little tract, "An Old Landmark Re-set," written by Pendleton and named and published by Graves in 1854, reveals the Baptist exclusivism which characterized Landmarkism. In his later years J. M. Pendleton refused to subscribe to some of the more extreme and dogmatic aspects of Landmarkism. But he helped to get the movement airborne, and he could be heard saying near the end of his life, "Baptists can never protest effectually against the errors of Pedobaptists which the preachers of the latter are recognized as gospel ministers. This to me is very plain." [5]

A. C. Dayton (1813–1865) was the third party in the Triumvirate. Converted from Presbyterian to Baptist views in 1852, Dayton joined forces with Graves and assumed a writing ministry. He is remembered primarily as the author of a religious novel, *Theodosia Ernest*, which depicts the true church and which is, of course, Baptist.

With less powerful personalities at the helm, Landmark ideas would have never gained the prominence they enjoyed. But these were strong, colorful men with a sense of mission and deep convictions. They crusaded to see their ideas accepted. J. R. Graves boasted in 1880 that only one out of sixteen Baptist newspapers in the South rejected basic tenets of Landmarkism. To say the least, Graves and his cohorts had been influential.

How or why did Landmarkism get such a firm toehold in Southern Baptist life? First, some of the emphases which the Landmark movement organized into such a tightly knit system antedate Landmarkism in Baptist life. Some of the Landmark teachings were not so much "innovations" as they were "intensifications" of Baptist ideas. Landmarkers perverted Baptist history via exaggeration. They affirmed that Baptists had always been Landmarkers. And as Baptist historians and theologians know, this was patently not the case.

Second, Landmarkism emerged in the context of some bitter denominational rivalries. These were the days of denominational debating, especially between Baptists and Methodists and Baptists and the followers of Alexander Campbell. J. R. Graves endeared himself to a number of his fellow Baptists early in his ministry as a great apologist for the denomination. They therefore followed him through the years.

Third, Landmarkism had a means of popularizing itself—through a Baptist newspaper of which Graves was editor. For some years following 1869, the *Tennessee Baptist* served as the official paper for Arkansas, Louisiana, and Mississippi, as well as for Tennessee. Graves had the media; he also had the market. Fourth, Graves was a capable man who persuaded others by his tremendous dedication to what he taught. The movement cannot be understood, in terms of its teaching or growth, apart from the man.

II

Above I said that Landmarkism was a "tightly knit system." And it was. And very tightly knitted. Ecclesiology, the doctrine of the church, was its consuming concern. What was the essence of the Landmark system? *The primacy of the local church.* "Church" to a Landmarker meant a local and visible and completely independent congregation of baptized (immersed) believers which could trace its history back to the time of Christ. Only Baptist churches were true churches. Organizations practicing non-Baptist ideas did not, therefore, fit into the category of a "true" church. And because non-Baptist organizations were not "true churches," only "religious societies," they had no authority to authorize a man to preach. Nor were their ordinances valid. Now with all this being true, as Landmarkers contended, what should be the Baptist attitude toward other denominations?

As a distinct movement within the Baptist tradition, Landmarkism began in 1851 at Cotton Grove, Tennessee. J. R. Graves submitted a series of five questions, later to be known as the "Cotton Grove Resolutions," which constituted the first official pronouncement of the Landmark movement.

To let you taste the flavor of Landmarkism, the "resolutions" are printed below. You will doubtless be able to tell that Graves answered all of the questions, with the exception of number four, with a resounding "no."

1st. Can Baptists consistently, with their principles or the scriptures, recognize those societies, not organized according to the pattern of the Jerusalem church, but possessing a different *government,* different *officers,* a different class of *membership,* different *ordinances, doctrines* and *practices,* as the Church of Christ?

2nd. Ought they to be called Gospel Churches or Churches in a religious sense?

3rd. Can we consistently recognize the ministers of such irregular and unscriptural bodies, as gospel ministers in their official capacity?

4th. Is it not virtually recognizing them as official ministers to invite them into our pulpits, or by any other act that would or could be construed into such a recognition?

5th. Can we consistently address as brethren, those professing Christianity, who not only have not the doctrines of Christ and walk not according to his commandments, but are arrayed in direct and bitter opposition to them?

In essence, these resolutions disavowed the authority of non-Baptist churches, ministers, and ordinances. The conclusions of the Cotton Grove Resolutions were clear to all: only Baptist churches are gospel churches! All other churches and denominations Graves labeled "religious societies."

Three years after the Cotton Grove meeting, J. M. Pendleton's famous essay, "An Old Landmark Re-set" hit the Landmark press. The next year, in 1855, the term "Landmark" was used for the first time on the floor of the Southern Baptist Convention. In that year the messengers to the Convention debated the propriety of permitting ministers from other denominations to "be invited to seats in the Convention, to aid by counsel and advice."

This was something which heretofore had not been an issue in the Southern Baptist Convention. Davis C. Woolley was right on target in saying, "These discussions related to the 'true church' and her ministers. This subject was at the heart of J. R. Graves' 'Old Landmark' doctrines." [7]

In 1880 J. R. Graves wrote the definitive work on his movement. It was entitled *Old Landmarkism: What Is It?* One of his major purposes in writing the book, he said, was "to establish the fact in the minds of all, who will give me an impartial hearing, that Baptist churches are the churches of Christ, and that they *alone* hold, and have alone ever held, and preserved the doctrine of the gospel in all ages since the ascension of Christ." [8]

Care should be taken in defining Landmarkism. Graves did not deny that there were Christians outside Baptist churches, even though his earlier statements such as the fifth Cotton Grove resolution came dangerously close to such an idea. For Graves the issue was "the true church," not spiritual regeneration. He believed that one must be a Christian before joining the true church ("Blood Before Water," he often said) and therefore there could be Christians outside the church. Debating a Methodist on one occasion, Graves said, "I wish one thing to be distinctly understood, i. e., the question is not whether the individual members of the Methodist Society here are *Christians* or not." [9] Graves claimed he was "unchurching" religious organizations, not "unchristianizing" the members of those organizations.

III

Landmark doctrines had some very practical implications for Baptist life. The first of these is seen in the extreme emphasis upon the local church. Baptists prior to Landmarkism, both in England and America, had always stressed the independence of local Baptist churches. But Landmarkers took this perfectly legitimate Baptist concept, blew it all out of proportion, and came dangerously close to making a fetish out of it. This is one example of the perversion via exaggeration referred to earlier.

Among other things, this meant that Landmarkism became gravely suspicious of all ecclesiastical boards beyond the local church level. Agencies which sought to coordinate the activities and ministries of the many individual Baptist churches came under suspicion. Mission boards and their authority for supervising missionary activities, for example, were eventually rejected by the more radical Landmarkers. They contended that only local churches had scriptural authority to examine, appoint, and supervise missionaries.

Landmark opposition to the "board method" of missions expressed itself on three distinct occasions in the Southern Baptist Convention.[10] The first was in 1859 at the meeting of the Southern Baptist Convention in Richmond, Virginia. Several months before the Convention J. R. Graves declared that "no man has lower views of the authority of a Missionary Board . . . than we have." And he thought the audacity of the Foreign Board to examine the religious experience of prospective missionaries was "a high-handed act."

A compromise resolution settled the issue in 1859, with the Foreign Mission Board left intact. But the anti-Conventionism and anti-Boardism of Landmarkism re-surfaced between 1885–1893 in a movement known as "Gospel Missionism." Several factors converged to form Gospel Missionism, but ideologically the movement continued the Landmark opposition against mission boards. Once again, however, the missionary methods of the Southern Baptist Convention survived.

Finally, and inevitably, the split came. A new Baptist denomination was born out of protest. Those whose emphasis on the local church excluded cooperation through Convention-wide boards organized the Baptist General Association in Texarkana, Arkansas. Ben Bogard, the leader of the newly formed group, once wrote concerning "the thirteen evils of conventionism." His considered conclusion: "A Convention is unknown to the Scriptures . . . and should not be tolerated by the churches." [11]

Bogard's group was thoroughly Landmarkist. Not only in their sentiment of anti-boardism but also in their Baptist exclusivism they continued the emphasis of J. R. Graves. One of their early leaders wrote, "Why, it is patent as the day that the only true churches of Jesus Christ in the world today are landmark Baptist churches." [12]

The Landmark Baptists continue to the present. In 1924 the name was changed from the Baptist General Association to the American Baptist Association. What was the effect of the Landmark attack on the missionary operations? Some think Southern Baptists came out of the fray more committed than ever before to their missionary methodology. With the exit of the Landmarkers, Southern Baptists were unified in their approach to doing missions.

But organization of a distinct Landmark denomination did not mean the total elimination of Landmark influence on the Southern Baptist Convention. In his emphasis upon the church as being *local*, Graves also insisted that the church was totally *visible*. This was in contrast to the idea of an "invisible" or "universal" church which would include more than a local congregation of believers.

J. M. Pendleton disagreed with Graves at this point. Also, most Baptist theology prior to Graves had little trouble defining the church as both local and universal, visible and invisible. Nevertheless, Graves' concept of the church found an audience among many Southern Baptists. It is interesting to note that when the Southern Baptist Convention approved a Confession of Faith in 1963, the only debate came on one sentence: "The New Testament speaks also of the church as the body of Christ which includes all of the redeemed of all ages." The statement was adopted, however.

So, Landmarkism, with its emphasis on the local and visible nature of the church, continued to affect Baptists of the South. A second characteristic of Landmarkism was its peculiar interpretation of Baptist history. Claiming that Jesus established a visible kingdom, that *true* churches constitute that kindgom, and that the kingdom has always existed (because Jesus said it would never perish), Graves logically concluded that the *true* churches have had an unbroken historical succession leading back to New Testament times. And remember, *true* churches are *Baptist* churches!

You can understand why this has been named the "Jerusalem-Jordan-John" theory of Baptist beginnings. And if one accepts this view, you also understand why he insists that Baptists are not Protestants. Baptists, unlike Protestants, it is argued, did not "protest" against the Roman Catholic and form a new church. Baptists, according to this view, pre-date the Protestant Reformation and Roman Catholicism. You also recognize this to be the theory of Baptist history which W. H. Whitsitt opposed. The Whitsitt Controversy, discussed in chapter one, is an outgrowth of Landmarkism.

A third inevitable result of Landmark teachings was that some Baptists hardened their attitude toward ministers of other denominations. The "Cotton Grove Resolutions" and Pendleton's important tract, "An Old Landmark Re-set," were both concerned with the belief that Baptists should not acknowledge ministers of other denominations as "official" gospel ministers. Specifically, and practically, this meant Baptists should not invite non-Baptist ministers to preach in Baptist pulpits. And baptism, even if immersion, is not legitimate if performed by a non-Baptist minister.

The Landmark Baptists who formed their own denomination in 1905 have perpetuated the policy of isolationism toward other denominations. Within the Southern Baptist Convention this reserve toward other religious groups has also been present, though not as extreme. Landmarkism is not the only explanation for this reservation among Southern Baptists. But it certainly is an important influence.

The fourth area where Landmarkism helped shape Southern Baptist ideas has to do with the ordinances. As indicated earlier, Landmarkers rejected "alien immersion" because it was performed in a non-Baptist church by a non-Baptist minister. "Alien immersion" was also rejected because of what Landmarkers called its irregular "design" or purpose. This was especially true in relation to the Church of Christ, which taught that baptism was a necessary step in salvation.

Even before the rise of Landmarkism, Baptists were divided over the validity of "alien immersion." However, there was no unanimity on the matter. The error of Landmarkism was in distorting Baptist history and claiming that all Baptists once denounced alien immersion.

Southern Baptists still debate the validity of "alien immersion." What about it? Should a man who has been immersed in the name of the Trinity as a believing adult in a Methodist Church be accepted by a Baptish church? Or should the Baptists "re-baptize" him? One of Southern Baptists' most informed students of Baptist history said, "To be consistent with the heritage of Baptists, the judgment of the validity of non-Baptist baptism should be made by each congregation, and that without censure from fellow Baptists." [13]

The Lord's Supper is another area where a trace of Landmarkism may be seen in some Southern Baptist churches.

Reasoning that only Baptist baptism is valid baptism and that baptism is a prerequisite to the Lord's Table, Landmarkers followed the policy often described as "closed communion" or "strict communion." As with alien immersion, closed communion has, at times, been a hotly debated issue in Baptist history. English Baptists, in particular, can supply "big" Baptist names to support either side of the issue. Charles Spurgeon, for example, practiced "open communion" in his church.

In America, however, Baptists have been more uniform in their practice. Here "the almost unanimous practice of Baptists has been closed communion." [14] But Graves went further than to deny the Lord's Supper to people of other denominations. He said that only members of the local Baptist church administering the supper partake of communion. A Baptist could not take communion in any but his local church! This type of restricted communion was not followed by all of Graves' followers. Nor has it influenced Southern Baptist practice to any great extent. Many Southern Baptist churches continue to practice "closed communion" with regard to other denominations. On the other hand, a number of Southern Baptist churches gladly welcome all Christians to the Lord's Table.

There is no single Southern Baptist "position" on the issue. In 1966 at the Southern Baptist Convention in Detroit, a messenger from an Arkansas church protested the seating of messengers from the First Baptist Church, Russellville, Arkansas, and moved that they be denied official seats in the Convention because the church has adopted a doctrinal statement advocating the practice of open communion and the acceptance of alien immersion.

Wayne Dehoney, President of the Convention, ruled the motion out of order and gave three reasons for his ruling: (1) The Constitution of the Southern Baptist Convention does not make these two matters a condition for seating messengers in the Convention; (2) the "Baptist Faith and Message" adopted in 1963 does not declare a position on these matters; and (3) traditionally and historically the Convention has never made these matters a test of fellowship. The Convention accepted Dehoney's ruling without objection.[15]

To some degree, one could say that the ghost of J. R. Graves was at that Convention. And he was ruled out of order! Without question, Landmarkism is one of the most significant developments in the life of Baptists in America.

NOTES

1. Hugh Wamble, "Landmarkism: Doctrinaire Ecclesiology Among Baptists," (*Church History*, December, 1964) p. 429.

2. O. L. Hailey, *J. R. Graves: Life, Times and Teachings*, (Nashville, Tennessee, n. p.,) p. 44.

3. J. M. Pendleton, *Reminiscences of a Long Life* (Louisville, Kentucky, Press Baptist Book Concern, 1891) p. 103.

4. *Ibid.*, pp. 103, 104.

5. *Ibid.*, p. 105.

6. As quoted in William Wright Barnes, *The Southern Baptist Convention, 1845–1953*, (Nashville: Broadman Press, 1954) p. 104.

7. Davis C. Woolley, "Major Convention Crises Over a Century and a Quarter," (*Review and Expositor*, Spring, 1970) p. 167. See John A. Broadus, *Memoir of James Petigru Boyce* (New York: A. C. Armstrong and Son, 1893) pp. 98–99.

8. As quoted in Robert A. Baker, *A Baptist Source Book with Particular Reference to Southern Baptists* (Nashville: Broadman Press, 1966) p. 142.

9. *The Graves-Ditzler Debate* (Memphis: Southern Baptist Publication Society, 1876) p. 927. See also *Old Landmarkism: What Is It?* in Baker, *op. cit.,* p. 144.

10. See the excellent summary article, David L. Saunders, "The Relation of Landmarkism to Mission Methods," (*The Quarterly Review,* vol. 26, no. 2, 1966) pp. 43–57.

11. See *Ibid.,* p. 56.

12. As quoted by John E. Steely, "The Landmark Movement in the Southern Baptist Convention," in Duke K. McCall, editor, *What Is the Church?* (Nashville, Broadman Press, 1958) p. 142.

13. W. Morgan Patterson, "The Role of Baptism in Baptist History," (*Review and Expositor,* Winter, 1968) p. 39.

14. W. Morgan Patterson, "The Lord's Supper in Baptist History," (*Renew and Expositor,* Winter, 1969) p. 32.

15. *Southern Baptist Convention Annual,* 1966, p. 47.

The "What Must Baptists Believe?" Controversy

or

Baptists Argue About Theology

"The world broke in two in 1922 or thereabouts," said Willa Cather. Not literally, it didn't. But the world in general, and America in particular was certainly busy trying to plug the holes created by the gushing currents of change. It really looked like everything nailed down was coming loose.

Life had not been the same since the middle of the nineteenth century. It would never be the same. Immigration had changed America's religion: from "Protestant Empire" to religious pluralism. Industrialization changed her vocation: from farmer to factory hand. Urbanization changed her home: from pasture to pavement.

But by 1922—to use the novelist's date again—nothing had undergone the challenge of change as much as the ideas men lived by. There had been Intellectual Revolution afoot! Freud challenged man's way of relating to self; Marx, his way of relating to others; and Darwin, his way of relating to nature.

With change comes controversy. That is an inexorable law of human history. The church, as all other institutions of society, eyeballed change. For some, it was "love at first sight." Willing to marry the present and forget the past, they became known as "Modernists." For others, it was cautious flirtation. They liked some of what they saw in Change, but the Past was still attractive, too. You can label them "Conservatives" or "Progressive Conservatives" or "Conservative Modernists," depending where you want your emphasis. But still there were others, and for them Change was viewed not as a lover but a Bandit. She was trying to steal what was lovely and fundamental in life. So you can call these "Fundamentalists." These are general terms and dangerous ones, because as someone said they can too easily degenerate from labels into libels; but they give us a starting point.

Is there any wonder, then, that in the 1920's American Protestantism experienced what church historians now call the Fundamentalist-Modernist controversy? There is a real sense in which many American churches "broke in two" during this controversy. And "1922 or thereabouts" is as good a date as any, if you just have to have a date.[1]

I

Baptists were not exempt from the combat. In the late nineteenth and early twentieth centuries, they were racked by theological fist-fights. This was true of English Baptists, American (Northern) Baptists, Canadian Baptists, and Southern Baptists. Each of these groups had its own unique controversy, but underneath much of the yelling and name-calling were two basic issues: scientific evolution and biblical interpretation.

While our primary concern here is with Southern Baptists, one can better interpret and appreciate their conflict in the context of the battles of their denominational kinsmen. The English Baptist argument is known as "The Downgrade Controversy." Principal antagonists were two of the tallest spirits British Baptists have ever produced. It was Charles Haddon Spurgeon vs. John Clifford.

Spurgeon, a man who once bragged of smoking cigars to the glory of God, was one of the greatest preachers ever to mount a Christian platform. One minister described him as "the sauciest dog that ever barked in a pulpit." His sermons are still read—and preached! Clifford, a great preacher in his own right, was known primarily for his denominational statesmanship and his leadership in social reform. He was the first president of the Baptist World Alliance. Both Spurgeon and Clifford were warm spirited and devout Christian men.

Charles Spurgeon suspected heresy of creeping into Baptist ranks, and he accused certain unnamed pastors of initiating "a new religion which was no more Christianity than chalk was cheese." He called for Baptists to adopt a written creed to protect the denomination. British Baptists rejected his plea for a binding doctrinal statement, accepted his resignation from the British Baptist Union in 1887, and expressed disapproval of his issuing general accusations without spelling out the alleged heretics.

Believing firmly in the inspiration and authority of the Bible but never wanting to repress the freedom to reinterpret the Bible, Clifford led the resistance to Spurgeon. The Downgrade Controversy is representative of a number of honest Baptist struggles. Spurgeon wanted orthodoxy, even if it meant restriction of some freedom of thought. Clifford wanted liberty, even if it meant the presence of what some believed to be unorthodox teaching.

Writing a half century after the controversy, one British historian said, "After more than fifty years, few, if any, Baptists are now other than thankful that the Union took the stand it did and refused Spurgeon's demand that it should accept a definite creed in place of its Declaration of Faith." [2] While British Baptists refused Spurgeon at this one point, they did not forget him or fail to enshrine him in their history. A life-size bronze statue of the great preacher was placed in the denominational headquarters.

English churchmen were in fraternal combat in the last part of the nineteenth century, but the Fundamentalist-Modernist battle brewing in North America made the English conflict look like a Sunday afternoon picnic. Wayne E. Ward defined Fundamentalism as "an ultraconservative theological movement, and sometimes a reactionary religious attitude, which has cut across many denominations and affected all parts of Christendom." [3] Fundamentalism's archenemy was Modernism. Denying biblical literalism, biblical inerrancy, and biblical infallibility, Modernism wanted to reformulate traditional theological concepts and make them more amenable to the modern scientific mind. This could be done, they contended, without sacrificing the religious truth of the Christian faith.

Fundamentalism, like Modernism, was a theological centipede. It had many different branches, so any attempt at generalizing gets you into historically muddy water. But there are three events in Fundamentalism which help cast light on the movement. First, between the years 1910–1912 a series of twelve small paperback volumes entitled *The Fun-*

damentals: A Testimony to the Truth were published. Financed by two wealthy California laymen, this set was to be sent free of charge to "every pastor, evangelist, missionary, theological student, Sunday School superintendent, Y. M. C. A. and Y. W. C. A. secretary in the English speaking world." [4] Eventually around three million copies were printed. In his book on *The History of Fundamentalism*, Stewart G. Cole said that in the publication of these books "the historian finds the clear emergence of fundamentalism."

The Fundamentals stressed what has often been called the Five Points of Fundamentalism. And while these Five Points constitute a gross oversimplification of the movement, they do point to the common beliefs of fundamentalists. The Five Points were: (1) Divinely inspired and inerrant Scriptures, (2) Deity of Christ and Virgin Birth, (3) The substitutionary atonement, (4) Christ's bodily resurrection, and (5) His personal, premillennial, and imminent second coming. Writing articles in *The Fundamentals* were at least three Southern Baptists—J. J. Reeve and Charles B. Williams of Southwestern Seminary in Fort Worth and E. Y. Mullins, president of Southern Baptist Theological Seminary in Louisville, Kentucky.

A second important event which helped solidify the Fundamentalism movement was the formation in 1919 of the World's Christian Fundamentals Association. Over 6,500 leaders gathered in Philadelphia to launch an effort to save American churches from the menace of Modernism and especially from the evolutionary concepts of Charles Darwin. Northern Baptists, Canadian Baptists, and Southern Baptists eventually provided strong leaders for the Association.

Without a doubt the most memorable religious event in America in the 1920's was the Scopes Monkey Trial held in 1925 in the sleepy little town of Dayton, Tennessee. This is the third event which highlights the religious conflict of this era. John Thomas Scopes, a high school coach and substitute biology teacher, was accused and tried for violating the state's recently enacted anti-evolution law which prohibited the teaching of the scientific theory in the classroom.

The trial pitted William Jennings Bryan, prosecutor and Presbyterian Fundamentalist, against Clarence Darrow, defense attorney and agnostic. Dayton virtually became a three-ring circus. In fact, there were enough dramatics present in the trial to make it a Broadway play, *Inherit the Wind*, and later a movie by the same name.

Between 1921–1927 thirty-seven anti-evolution measures were introduced in twenty state legislatures. Only five won approval. These were in Tennessee, Oklahoma, Florida, Mississippi, and Arkansas. The battle of evolution, being fought in legislatures, courts, and public schools, was also being fought in the churches of America. The relationship between religion and science, and the corollary issue of biblical authority, posed the battleground.

This was the background for the conflict among Baptists in North America. Canadian Baptists and Northern Baptists were more directly affected, in terms of denominational division, than were Southern Baptists. Among Canadian Baptists the Fundamentalist movement was spearheaded by T. T. Shields, pastor of the Jarvis Street Church in Toronto, and directed primarily against alleged Modernism at McMaster University, the Baptist owned school. By the end of 1927 the Ontario-Quebec Baptist Convention had excluded Jarvis

Street church from the denomination. Shields then organized the Union of Regular Baptist Churches. Baptists in Central Canada have been divided ever since.[5]

Baptists in the Northern United States also divided during the Fundamentalist-Modernist controversy. W. B. Riley, pastor of First Baptist Church in Minneapolis, led the fight for Fundamentalism; while the most renowned "Modernist" was Harry Emerson Fosdick, once described as "the Jesse James of the theological world."

Northern Baptist Fundamentalists made several efforts to restrain what was considered destructive theological tendencies. First, they demanded that Northern Baptist colleges and seminaries be investigated for Modernist teachings. The investigation was made and the schools exonerated in 1921. Second, in 1922 Riley tried to persuade the Northern Baptist Convention to adopt a confession of faith to insure doctrinal uniformity. But in the place of a clear-cut doctrinal statement, Northern Baptists adopted a resolution stating "that the New Testament is the all-sufficient ground of our faith and practice, and we need no other." [6] When a third effort failed, directed this time against the Foreign Missionary Society, some of the more conservative Northern Baptists withdrew to form a new Baptist body.

II

Modernism never strutted in the South as it had in the North. For Southern Baptists, this meant that the Fundamentalist-Modernist controversy was not as grave an issue as it had been among Northern Baptists. But there was tension. And there would be separation, but it would be small.

Numbered among those Southern Baptists who could be called leading Fundamentalists were such men as T. T. Martin of Mississippi, C. P. Stealey of Oklahoma, and John W. Porter of Kentucky. Concerned primarily with what they considered Modernist teachings, and especially evolution, they took constant pot-shots at Baptist schools and professors.

While these men spelled trouble for the harmony of the Southern Baptist Convention, Southern Baptists had one Fundamentalist among them who, in terms of sensational tactics, vituperative rhetoric, and pulpit dramatics, possessed no rival, North or South. He was J. Frank Norris, pastor of the First Baptist Church of Fort Worth, Texas.

Before the civil courts of Texas, Norris was indicted for arson, tried for perjury, and acquitted on a murder charge! The state Baptist Convention of Texas censored him in 1922, refused a seat to a delegate from his church in 1923, and expelled him and his church from the Texas Convention in 1924. He was a forceful, dynamic preacher and a rare bird who loved to fly in the fires of controversy.

J. Frank Norris became pastor of First Church in Fort Worth in 1909 and remained there until his death in 1952. When he was called to the Fort Worth pastorate, only one family voted against him out of the three hundred and thirty-four people who voted. The deacon who voted "no" explained his vote before the church:

"I am not opposed to J. Frank Norris; I am for him but this church is in no condition for his type of ministry. If he comes, there will be the allfiredest explosion ever witnessed in any church. We are at peace with the world, the flesh, the devil, and with one another. And this fellow carries a broad axe and not a pearl handled pen-knife. I just want to warn you." [7]

"This fellow carries a broad axe!" How absolutely apt for
J. Frank Norris!

He carried "a broad axe" within his local church fellowship. And while the church had serious internal strife and
overt division, the congregation also knew phenomenal
growth. From a membership of 900 in 1911, by 1928 the
church increased to 12,000 members, with 5,200 average
attendance in Sunday School. Most of the growth of the
church has been attributed to the individual sensationalism
of Norris.

He carried "a broad axe" to city hall, accusing political
officials of corruption, graft, and immorality. Dr. Norris
preached a sermon on July 11, 1926, in which he described
the mayor of Fort Worth and his associates as a "two by four,
simian-headed, sawdust-brained, bunch of grafters." He accused his enemies of "tampering with the wires" of his radio
station and declared that "some of you low down devils that
monkey around this property, arrange for your undertaker
before you come around here." To an applauding congregation he announced that his guards would "shoot to kill." [8]

The next Saturday a friend of the mayor's, a lumberman
by the name of D. C. Chipps, entered the pastor's study and
an argument followed. Two hours later newspaper boys ped-
dled extra editions of their papers with headlines reading:
"D. E. Chipps, Lumberman, Slain by J. Frank Norris." That
was July 17, 1926. The next January the pastor was acquitted
in a Texas court on the grounds of self-defense.

Norris also carried "a broad axe" into denominational
struggles. In October, 1921, a Fort Worth newspaper carried
this terse advertisement: "Sunday night Dr. Norris will ex-
pose infidelity in Baylor University." The next Sunday night

he gave the Baptist school in Waco a thorough tongue-lashing. "With a flowing tide of words, with violent gestures and the poise of righteous indignation, he proceeded to cry that compromise, modernism, complacency, and infidelity were undermining the fortress of the Baptist faith in the South —Baylor University at Waco." [9]

Through his newspaper, *The Searchlight,* the fiery preacher continued to focus on Baylor University. Norris was expecially concerned about a sociology professor whose book, according to Norris, advocated evolution and rejected inspiration of Scripture. In 1921 the Texas Baptist Convention appointed a committee to investigate the charges against Baylor. Norris lost his battle as Baylor was given the approval of the state Convention. Nonetheless, by 1923 Professor Dow had departed from Baylor.

Norris kept fighting Baylor and his denomination in general. In 1923 he said, "I intend to start a fight on evolution and on the denomination and I never expect to stop until it is extracted, root and branch, and if the denomination is split, it will split over the question of evolution." [10] But by this time Norris had already run into the ire of his denominational brethren. His local Baptist association excluded his church in 1922, primarily for his censoriousness and non-cooperation.

He was having a running battle with several of the most respected men among Texas Baptists: George W. Truett of First Baptist Church in Dallas; J. M. Dawson, pastor of First Church in Waco; and L. R. Scarborough, president of Southwestern Seminary. Dr. Scarborough would eventually write a stinging little tract entitled "The Fruits of Norrism." Scarborough called "Norrism" "an old cult under a new name," and among several other demonic characteristics said "it thrives on sensationalism, misrepresentation and false accusations of good men and true causes. It masquerades under the cloak of anti-evolution, anti-modernism, anti-catholicism in order to ride into public favor and cast poisonous suspicion on the leadership of constructive Christianity." [11] The brethren were battling!

But if Norris had problems finding acceptance among leading Southern Baptists, he did not lack for friends in Fundamentalist circles beyond his denomination. Especially had Norris come to know and admire the work of T. T. Shields and W. B. Riley. And the admiration was mutual. The three of them constituted a Baptist Fundamentalist triumvirate in North America—Shields in Canada, Riley among Northern Baptists and Norris in the South.

Together they had led in the formation of the World's Christian Fundamentals Association in 1919. In 1922 Shields, Norris and Riley issued a "Call and Manifesto" to the Baptist clergy of Canada and the United States. In response to the call the Baptist Bible Union of North America was organized in May, 1923 at Kansas City. The purpose of the union was "to give the people the fullest information respecting the ravages of Modernism in all departments of . . . denominational life." [12]

Thus there was born a Pan-Baptist Fundamentalist organization for North America. It was strong and vocal, harrassing all major Baptist denominations until about 1927. By 1930 the original organization had died.

III

With men like Norris firmly committed to purging Southern Baptists of heresy, and with the agitation that came from organizations like the Baptist Bible Union of North America, and with the widespread caution on the part of moderate men concerning the new scientific theories, it was inevitable that the issues ultimately would appear on the floor of the Southern Baptist Convention. They did.

And yet one has difficulty describing the conflict of the 20's among Southern Baptists as the Fundamentalist-Modernist Controversy. The reason is that there were apparently few, if any, confirmed Modernists among Southern Baptists. There were some open to the new science, but the vast majority of Southern Baptists accepted the theology of Fundamentalism. What they were reluctant to accept was the constant carping and the effort at denominational domination by the more radical Fundamentalists.

Nevertheless, throughout the 1920's the Southern Baptist Convention, in formal sessions, addressed itself to the relationship of science and religion. When the Convention met in 1922 at Jacksonville, Florida, the committee reporting for the Education Board issued two cautions to Southern Baptists. First, the committee warned that "great care should be exercised lest, by innuendo and nebulous criticism, the minds of the people be weaned away from loyalty to their schools" and "indiscriminate criticism is not the best way to correct an error in an individual or school." This was, obviously, a move to counter the attacks which were already being launched by men like Norris.

"But this should not be the end of caution," the report continued. The education institutions of Southern Baptists were urged "not to use the textbooks in their curriculum which are calculated to undermine the faith of the students in the Bible." The profound conviction of the reporting committee was that one could not "understand the Bible and believe both the Bible and the accepted theory of evolution" as set forth in some science textbooks.

The 1922 messengers were further reminded of President E. Y. Mullins' annual sermon and the applause he received from the Convention when he said:

We have been much concerned over modern rationalism and the false assumptions of materialistic science . . . . It seems to me three things are clear, First, we will not tolerate in our denominational schools any departure from the great fundamentals of the faith in the name of science falsely so-called. Second, we will not be unjust to our teachers, nor curtail unduly their God-given right to investigate truth in the realm of science. Firm faith and free research is our noble Baptist ideal. Third, we will be loyal to every fact which is established in any realm of research, just as we are loyal to the supreme fact of Christ, His virgin birth, His sinless life, His atoning death, His resurrection and present reign.

Obviously, President Mullins was trying to steer the Convention on a middle course as he described "firm faith and free research" as "our noble Baptist ideal." [13]

The next year, 1923, E. Y. Mullins entitled his presidential address to the Convention, "Present Dangers and Duties." He evidently hoped to calm the waters by speaking publicly to the issue once again. He reiterated the refrain of "free research" but protested against unestablished scientific theories parading as confirmed facts. Also, he echoed, in a more elaborate and arousing presentation, the emphasis on "a firm faith." After stating what he considered to be the basic "supernatural elements in the Christian religion," he said that adherence to these truths is "a necessary condition of service for teachers in our Baptist schools."

On the motion of a messenger from Oklahoma, that part of Dr. Mullins' address referring to "Science and Religion" was officially adopted as "the belief" of the Convention. But this did not go far enough for some of the brethren. J. F. Brownlow of Tennessee offered a resolution calling for the appointment of a committee which would cooperate with the trustees of all Baptist colleges "in bringing about the death" of evolutionary teaching on Baptist campuses. The resolution was rejected "on the ground of interference beyond the province of the Convention." Colleges and universities owned by state Baptist conventions could not be supervised by the Southern Baptist Convention.[14]

By the time the convention met in Atlanta in 1924, the controversy had intensified. An effort was now being made by the more extreme Fundamentalists to pressure the Convention into accepting a binding doctrinal statement. Motions by C. P. Stealey and R. K. Maiden to this effect were, however, rejected by the Convention. But in the name of peace-seeking a special committee was appointed "to consider the advisability of issuing another statement of the Baptist faith and message." The committee, chaired by E. Y. Mullins was to report to the 1925 Convention in Memphis.

Before the Convention met in Memphis, the Southern Baptist Educational Association, an organization of denominational educators, issued a statement cautioning church colleges to "avoid alliance with either Fundamentalism or Modernism." The Education Association also asserted that the "Bible cannot be taken literally and never was meant to be." In response, Mississippi Fundamentalist T. T. Martin proposed that the Southern Baptist Convention divide. "Let all who endorse . . . this stand taken by the Southern Baptist Educational Association go into one convention; let all who reject and repudiate this action go into the other convention." He warned if this were not done, "there is going to be fearful division and strife." [15]

Strife continued, but there was no "fearful division." The special committee presented its report to the Memphis Convention in 1925. The report consisted of a Confession of Faith (the Confession was a revision of the older New Hampshire Confession plus ten additional articles), a carefully worded preface on the meaning of confessions of faith, and a closing statement on "Science and religion" (this was a duplication of the Mullins statement adopted by the 1923 Convention).

Some individuals on the committee and others throughout the Convention obviously looked askance on the idea of a Confession of Faith, for the committee recommended the document with the qualifying words, "in the event a statement of the Baptist faith and message is deemed necessary at this time."

The Convention of 1925 deemed it necessary, because the Confession was adopted along with the rest of the committee's report. A part of that report, as mentioned above, was an introductory statement explaining the nature of Baptist Confessions of faith. This Convention affirmed that the articles of the Confession were not "complete statements of our faith, having any quality of finality or infallibility," but "they are statements of religious convictions, drawn from the Scriptures, and are not to be used to hamper freedom of thought or investigation in other realms of life."

As you shall see in the next chapter, the 1925 Memphis Confession was slightly revised and adopted by the Southern

Baptist Convention of Kansas City in 1963. Herschel H. Hobbs of Oklahoma was chairman of the committee which presented the 1963 Kansas City Confession. He underscored the fact that the introductory statements were as much a part of the overall statement as the articles of faith. And he added, "If this be denied or ignored, then the statement becomes a creed." [16] And Baptists are a non-creedal people.

While Baptists traditionally have opposed binding creeds, they have nonetheless adopted periodic "confessions" or "declarations" of their faith. Therefore the Southern Baptist Convention meeting in 1925 had ample denominational precedent for their actions. "The present occasion for a reaffirmation of Christian fundamentals," said the 1925 committee, "is the prevalence of naturalism in the modern teaching and preaching of religion." And they added, "We repudiate every theory of religion which denies the supernatural elements in our faith." E. Y. Mullins' hand is certainly present in those statements. In his previous statements he had carefully described the issue as supernaturalism versus naturalism. He avoided making the issue more specific, as between scientific evolution and the Bible.

By reading the committee's report, you could almost bet that one member of the committee, C. P. Stealey, was not satisfied. And he wasn't. Article 3 of the Confession was not specific enough for him. It read: "Man was created by the special act of God, as recorded in Genesis." On the Convention floor Stealey proposed the following amendment: "We believe man came into the world, by direct creation of God, and not by evolution. This creative act was separate and distinct from any other work of God and was not conditioned upon antecedent changes in previously created forms of life." [17] The amendment failed to pass and Article 3 of the Confession stood as presented.

Strife continued. The J. Frank Norris-C. P. Stealey wing of the Convention wanted a more explicit denial of the evolution theory than the Southern Baptist Convention had been willing to give. When the Convention met in Houston in 1926, George W. McDaniel, pastor of First Baptist Church in Richmond, Virginia, was president. He concluded a message to the Convention with the following words: "This Convention accepts Genesis as teaching that man was the special creation of God, and rejects every theory, evolution or other, which teaches that man originated in, or came by way of, a lower animal ancestry." [18]

M. E. Dodd, of First Baptist Church in Shreveport, Louisiana, moved that McDaniel's statement on the subject of evolution and the origin of man be adopted as the sentiment of the Convention. It was the most unambiguous statement the Convention had adopted on the issue, but the avid Fundamentalists were not finished. Even though Dodd's motion included the suggestion that no more attention be given to the evolution issue, more was to come.

On the fourth day of the Convention a messenger from Arkansas, S. E. Tull, secured the adoption of a resolution which called for all employees of Southern Baptist agencies and institutions to subscribe to the McDaniel statement. Little wonder that the headlines in J. Frank Norris' paper shouted: "SOUTHERN BAPTIST CONVENTION HEROICALLY AND TRIUMPHANTLY DELIVERS KNOCKOUT BLOW AGAINST EVOLUTION AND EVOLUTIONISTS."

Traces of the evolution controversy appeared for a couple of years. But after the Houston Convention, most of the umph of it all was gone. By the end of the decade Southern Baptists were not arguing over evolution. How or why did peace come? Peace came because the Norris-Stealey faction got what they wanted. The Convention spoke to the evolution problem, it spoke decisively, and it spoke what they wanted to hear. In a very real sense, the McDaniel statement amended Article 3 of the Memphis Confession of 1925.

The financial condition of the Southern Baptist Convention may have hastened harmony within the ranks. Just prior to the eruption of the evolution controversy, Southern Baptists adopted the Seventy-Five Million Campaign—an effort to raise 75 million dollars between 1919–1924. The campaign fell way short. Surely the controversy is not the only, not even the major, reason for the flop, but it was, doubtless, a contributing factor.

And, finally, peace came because of the growing disrepute of Fundamentalists like Norris. About two months after the 1926 Convention, Norris killed Chipps in his church office. Many Southern Baptists had already come to resent J. Frank Norris' hobby—"tending to the Convention." The Chipps incident did not elevate Norris in the eyes of the average Southern Baptist.

Debate, theological and otherwise, continues in Baptist circles. A good bet is that it always shall. How are we to evaluate this heritage: What can we learn? For one thing, we could learn to use cautiously such phrases as "the historic Baptist position." One is on safer ground with "the majority Baptist position." When one asks, "What do Baptists believe about such and such?" one must counter with "Which Baptists and in which period?"

The complexity and variety of Baptist thought is one reason, I suppose, why Baptist scholars have never written a book entitled *Baptist Theology*. If Baptists were a people who had tied their souls to a permanent creed, Baptist thought would be easier to delineate. At least three basic ideas have contributed to the diversity in Baptist life. One is the emphasis on the freedom of the individual. A second is the idea of congregational church government. And third, Baptists have made a lot out of "the leadership of the Spirit of God." Diversity and freedom are inherent in that idea.

Another thing about Baptist life: debate is possible. No single voice, however so informed, illiterate, or influential can stifle dissent in a democratic body. That there are problems in such a free-wheeling approach is obvious. But it is a logical outgrowth of the concept of individual worth and freedom.

Thirdly, we need to be reminded that oxthopraxy (right practice) is every bit as important as orthodoxy (right teaching). A man who believes right and shouts down a brother is wrong, no matter what he believes. And last of all, we would do well to remind ourselves that "majority rule" does not necessarily produce the will of God.

NOTES

1. For an excellent background discussion of the Fundamentalist-Modernist Controversy see especially pages 3–46 of Willard B. Gatewood, Jr., *Controversy in the Twenties: Fundamentalism, Modernism and Evolution,* (Nashville: Vanderbilt University Press, 1969).

2. A. C. Underwood, *A History of the English Baptists,* (London: The Carey Kingsgate Press, 1947), p. 230.

3. See article on "Fundamentalism" in *Encyclopedia of Southern Baptists,* volume 1, pp. 515, 516.

4. See Norman F. Furniss, *The Fundamentalist Controversy, 1918–1931*, (New Haven, Connecticut: Yale University Press, 1954), p. 12. These 12 volumes with slight omissions were reprinted in a four-volume edition issued by the Bible Institute of Los Angeles in 1917. The four volume edition was reprinted in 1970 by Baker Book House, Grand Rapids, Michigan.

5. For the Canadian Baptist Controversy see G. Gerald Harrop's article in Davis C. Woolley, editor, *Baptist Advance* (Nashville: Broadman Press, 1964), pp. 170–173.

6. As quoted in Robert G. Torbet, *A History of the Baptists* (Valley Forge, Pennsylvania: The Judson Press, Revised edition, 1963), p. 430. Torbet introduces one to the controversy among Northern Baptists as does Furniss, *op. cit.*,

7. As quoted in E. Ray Tatum, *Conquest or Failure: Biography of J. Frank Norris*, (Dallas, Texas: Baptist Historical Foundation, 1966), p. 102.

8. This account is in Kenneth K. Bailey, *Southern White Protestantism in the Twentieth Century*, (New York: Harper and Row), p. 61.

9. Tatum, p. 182.

10. As quoted in Tatum, p. 198.

11. As quoted in Robert A. Baker, *A Baptist Source Book With Particular Reference to Southern Baptists*, (Nashville: Broadman, 1966), p. 197.

12. See Stewart G. Cole, *The History of Fundamentalism*, (Harper and Row, 1931, reprinted by Archon Books, Hamden, Connecticut, 1963), p. 283.

13. For quotes in this section see *Southern Baptist Convention Annual*, 1922, pp. 35, 36.

14. For quotes see *Southern Baptist Convention Annual*, 1923, pp. 19, 20, 46, 62, 63.

15. As quoted in Bailey, pp. 65, 66.

16. Herschel H. Hobbs, *The Baptist Faith and Message* (Nashville: Convention Press, 1971), p. 12.

17. *Southern Baptist Convention Annual*, 1925, p. 76.

18. *Southern Baptist Convention Annual*, 1926, p. 18.

The
"What About Genesis?"
Controversy
or
Baptists Argue About
the Bible

Controversy is not something which has happened to Southern Baptists in the past. It is a happening of the present. In fact, no single decade of Southern Baptist history has spawned more serious controversy than the last ten years. During this period we have argued about many things, but mostly we have argued about biblical interpretation, especially the book of Genesis.

In the early 1960's Southern Baptists were preoccupied with the Elliott Controversy. In the very last months of 1969 and the early 1970's it was the Broadman Commentary Controversy. Both of these controversies focus on biblical and theological interpretation. Specifically, divergent interpretations of the book of Genesis constitute the major area of disagreement. While the Elliott and the Broadman Commentary controversies rocked Southern Baptists within the same ten-year period, and while the book of Genesis constituted the storm center of both battles, they are nonetheless distinct controversies. You should look at them separately. Only then can you adequately compare and contrast them.

I

Dr. Ralph H. Elliott is presently the pastor of an American Baptist church in Albany, New York. He was once a Southern Baptist and Professor of Old Testament at Midwestern Baptist Theological Seminary in Kansas City. He wrote a book which ignited a controversy among Southern Baptists. The controversy eventually let to the dismissal of Elliott from his teaching post.

Entitled *The Message of Genesis,* Elliott's book was, as he stated in his preface, "an effort to combine head and heart by using the sound achievements of modern scholarship to ferret out and to underscore the foundational theological and religious principles of the stories of Genesis." He wanted to skirt the twin dangers of a heartless scholarship and a headless religion.

Broadman Press, the book publishing arm of Southern Baptists' Sunday School board, released 4,000 copies of the book in July, 1961—in the heat of the year. Was the temperature an omen of things to come? Surely not. But one great big fire of a controversy came from the publication of the book. Criticism toward Elliott's biblical interpretation came quickly. Some Baptist editors, pastors, and state denominational workers exposed what they considered to be the liberal theology of Elliott.

In an interview six years after the controversy, Elliott was asked which part of the book received the most criticism. He answered, "My comments about the first eleven chapters of

Genesis, in which I suggested we are dealing with theological fact, not day-by-day physical history." And when asked what were some of the key questions which he raised in the book, the ex-professor said, "the seven days of creation. The most bitter critics felt God created the earth in seven literal 24-hour days. I just cannot buy this. And there was a question of whether Adam was just one man, or if he represents mankind. I raised the possibility the answer was mankind." [1]

Whereas Professor Elliott considered Genesis 1–11 (the story of creation, of Adam, the garden, the flood, the tower, etc.) symbolic, his critics insisted upon the literal and historical nature of these accounts. And whereas Elliott felt that the essential message of the Genesis (note the title of his book) material was not diminished but enriched by a symbolic interpretation, his opponents believed the trustworthiness of the Bible depended on the historical accuracy of the material. To be sure, these were not the only issues of dispute, but they were among the most commonly mentioned areas of disagreement.

Pointing out what he considered to be the gravity of the situation, one critic, writing in the September 9, 1961, issue of the Kansas *Baptist Digest*, said: "Southern Baptists are at the crossroads in the publication of this book. In this book we are not facing a matter of ecclesiology or polity. This concerns the very heart of the gospel. It is an undercutting of the doctrine of revelation." Many Southern Baptists agreed.

One of the most publicized criticisms of Elliott's book was published in the January 10, 1962, issue of *The Baptist Standard*, the Texas Baptist paper. K. Owen White, then pastor of First Baptist Church in Houston, wrote the article which he entitled, ". . . Death in the Pot." After quoting several passages from Elliott's work, White described it as "liberalism, pure and simple." And then he added, "the book in question is 'poison.' This sort of rationalistic criticism can lead only to further confusion, unbelief, deterioration, and ultimately disintegration as a great New Testament denomination." White suggested that men of Elliott's viewpoint should be invited to find a place of service outside Southern Baptist life. He also asked trustees of the seminaries to exercise caution in approving faculty members, and he urged the Sunday School Board to be more alert to liberalism in Baptist publications.

Elliott was not without support. Appearing in the same issue of *The Baptist Standard* alongside White's negative evaluation was a positive critique by Robert H. Craft, a Kansas pastor. In his highly complimentary view of Elliott's work Craft said, "The author leads the reader through an exhilarating and fruitful study of the delicate problems conservative scholars have too long neglected in the study of Genesis." One month later in the February 15 issue of the *Arkansas Baptist Newsmagazine*, Charles Trentham, pastor of First Baptist Church in Knoxville, Tennessee, praised Elliott's work for preserving "the true spiritual values of the Genesis narrative so that no honest student need feel that he is intellectually dishonest when he contends that there still is an honest harmony between science and religion."

In late 1961 the Board of Trustees at Midwestern Seminary passed a resolution affirming confidence in Elliott "as a consecrated Christian, a promising scholar and teacher, a loyal servant of Southern Baptists, and a dedicated and warmly evangelistic preacher of the gospel."

On the heels of the action by the Midwestern Board of Trustees, the 54 member Sunday School Board met in Nashville, January 29–31, 1962, for its semiannual meeting. A statement of position was adopted concerning the publication by Broadman Press of Elliott's book. The statement emphasized that *The Message of Genesis* was published for use as resource material for seminary students (one of the very things which critics of the book abhorred) and for in-depth Bible study.

Furthermore, the Sunday School Board stated that Broadman Press recognized that the point of view expressed in the book would not be acceptable to all Southern Baptists. But they contended that unanimity of acceptance was not a criteria for publication of a manuscript. The Sunday School Board urged Broadman Press, therefore, to continue to publish books which would present more than one point of view. And finally, the Sunday School Board declared that "Broadman Press ministers to the denomination in keeping with the historic Baptist principle of the freedom of the individual to interpret the Bible for himself, to hold a particular theory of inspiration of the Bible which seems most reasonable to him, and to develop his beliefs in accordance with his theory." [2]

But neither the praise which the pro-Elliott fans could muster nor the rationale given by the Sunday School Board could silence the issue. While it is impossible to know precisely how many Southern Baptists were "for" or "against" Elliott's viewpoints, the majority were undoubtably "against." Salvador T. Martinez made a careful study of the reactions of twenty-eight Southern Baptist newspapers and editors. Of the twenty-eight he said sixteen were unfavorable toward Elliott, five were favorable, four were uncommitted but would likely oppose Elliott, and three were uncommitted but would likely support Elliott.[3]

When Southern Baptists met for their annual convention in San Francisco in June, 1962, everybody knew that the big issue was "the Elliott thing." In March before the June Convention an informal group of Baptist pastors, denominational workers and laymen—critics of Elliott's book—met in Oklahoma City. They had met to discuss what they considered to be "the current theological crisis within the denomination." According to a March 16, 1962, Baptist Press news release, the "apparent immediate objective" of the group was to secure the election of theologically conservative men to the Board of Trustees of Midwestern Seminary.

This meeting was condemned by some Baptist editors, approved by others. Erwin L. McDonald of the *Arkansas Baptist Newsmagazine* objected by saying, "Surely we do not need anything that might remotely resemble a spiritual version of the Ku Klux Klan." And James F. Cole of the Louisiana paper, while not referring specifically to the Oklahoma meeting, warned his readers of the danger of "the society of authoritative dogmatism" as well as of "liberalism." But E. S. James of *The Baptist Standard* defended the meeting at Oklahoma City and decried the charge of Ku Kluxism.[4]

The Oklahoma City meeting represented the seriousness with which Southern Baptists were viewing the Elliott controversy. Prior to the 1962 San Francisco Convention Baptist papers were filled with articles examining every facet of the controversy. No one knew exactly what would happen at San Francisco. But the messengers arrived in the Bay Area expecting a showdown.

Before the four-day convention concluded, five resolutions were presented which related to Ralph Elliott, the seminaries' Boards of Trustees, and the Sunday School Board. The first of these was a recommendation presented by the Executive Committee of the Convention. It called for the appointment of a special committee to present a confessional statement, similar to the 1925 Memphis Confession, to the 1963 Southern Baptist Convention in Kansas City. Obviously some leaders hoped that the adoption of such a recommendation would de-fuse the Elliott bomb in San Francisco. The recommendation passed, the committee was appointed, but the fire was still not out.[5]

The second and third motions pertaining to the fuss were presented by K. Owen White of Houston. One of these, adopted unanimously, said: "That the messengers to this Convention, by standing vote, reaffirm their faith in the *entire* Bible as the authoritative, authentic, infallible Word of God." In the other White resolution, passed by a large majority, the messengers to the Convention declared:

That we express our abiding and unchanging objection to the dissemination of theological views in any of our seminaries which would undermine such faith in the historical accuracy and doctrinal integrity of the Bible, and that we courteously request the Trustees and administrative officers of our institutions and other agencies to take such steps as shall be necessary to remedy at once those situations where such views now threaten our historic position.[6]

A fourth motion presented by Ralph F. Powell of Missouri called for the Sunday School Board to stop publishing and "recall from all sales" *The Message of Genesis.* This motion was later withdrawn by Mr. Powell. Shortly after Powell withdrew his motion, a messenger from Oregon presented a similar proposal instructing "the Sunday School Board to cease publishing and to recall from all distribution channels, the book, *The Message of Genesis.*" The motion was defeated. So the Convention refused to ban Elliott's book. But the Sunday School Board, due to an administrative decision, never republished the book.

Following the San Francisco Convention, the complexion and attitude of Midwestern Seminary's Board of Trustees changed. Some obviously interpreted the action of the Southern Baptist Convention as a mandate to dismiss Elliott. A special committee of the board consulted with Elliott and the seminary administration. Agreement was reached concerning principles relating to biblical teaching, including the historical-critical method. The difference of opinion which led to Elliott's dismissal was over the republication of *The Message of Genesis.* The committee wanted Elliott to promise not to republish the book. He refused. He was then dismissed, not because of heresy, but because of insubordination.[7] As Davis C. Woolley said, "Elliott left Midwestern a victim of the controversy yet without the brand of a heretic." [8]

What were the results of the controversy? A couple are obvious. For one thing, a professor lost his job. Critics of Elliott saw it as a victory for theological conservatism; supporters of Elliott saw it as a tragic injustice. Secondly, Southern Baptists adopted a Confession of Faith in Kansas City in 1963. And yet, the adoption of the Confession was anticlimactic because Elliott was gone by the time of the 1963 Convention. A third and less obvious result of the discussion was an intensification and popularization of the suspicion of theological education and publications. A fourth result was that of a young seminary, established only in 1958, encountered a serious injury in its infancy.

II

Elliott left, but the problem remained. Only eight years after the stormy San Francisco Convention, Southern Baptists convened and had an even stormier session over Genesis. This time it was in Denver, Colorado, in June, 1970. The issue at stake was the recently published volume 1 of *The Broadman Bible Commentary*. The specific concern was the interpretation of the book of Genesis.

The Broadman Bible Commentary, a projected twelve-volume set of commentaries on the entire Bible, was conceived in 1957, approved by the elected Sunday School Board in 1961, and "designed for those who feel a need for a more thoughtful type of work, probing in depth into the truths of God's word." [9] Volume 1 of the commentary contained (1) general articles on the Bible, (2) an exposition of Genesis by G. Henton Davies, an English Baptist, (the Elliott Controversy may have helped the editors decide on a non-Southern Baptist writer for Genesis) and an exposition of Exodus by Roy L. Honeycutt, Professor of Old Testament at Midwestern Seminary.

Published in October, 1969, the commentary was expected to draw some criticism. In the September 11, 1969 issue of *The California Southern Baptist*, editor J. Terry Young issued a word of commendation and a word of caution even before volume 1 had been released. He commended the Sunday School Board and Broadman Press for publishing "this significant set." And then he added, "We don't know who will get to read the first copy off the press, but we confidently expect that he will find something in it with which he disagrees." But he argued that some diversity of interpretation is expected in the denomination because "that's the nature of us Baptists." He warned his readers that they would doubtless hear an assortment of criticisms of the commentaries. But he admonished individual Southern Baptists to form opinions on the basis of personal study and not the reaction of someone else.

Few, if any, anticipated as much dissatisfaction with the commentary as was finally expressed at the Denver Convention. State Baptist papers began editorializing and carrying articles and reviews of the commentary. Responses to the commentary varied; some applauded, others were cautious, and still others were decidedly negative.

One of the earliest published criticisms of volume 1 of the Broadman Commentary came from W. Ross Edwards, editor of *Word and Way,* the Missouri Baptist paper. In the January 8, 1970 issue of his paper, Edwards wrote an editorial entitled "Witnessing to the Truth," which he described as "Part 1 of a review of the Broadman Bible Commentary." He declared that the two recently released volumes of the Broadman Commentary were "well written and, in the main, conservative." But Edwards went on to say "that the writings of Dr. G. Henton Davies in the volume on Genesis are too liberal for most Southern Baptists."

Edwards' major criticism of Davies was in the English scholar's interpretation of Genesis 22:1–19, the story of Abraham's proposed sacrifice of Isaac. In his discussion of the passage, Davies acknowledged that some interpreters accepted literally the command to Abraham to sacrifice Isaac. Davies queried, "Did God make, would God in fact have made, such a demand upon Abraham or anybody else, except himself?" Davies then answered the question with the following paragraph

Our answer however is no. Indeed what Christian or humane conscience could regard such a command as coming from God? How then did this conviction arise in the mind of Abraham, since we believe that God did not put it there? The question can only be answered in part. Abraham's conviction that his son must be sacrificed is the climax of the psychology of his life.[10]

This became the most widely disputed intepretation in the commentary, and Edwards was one of the first to attack it. Edwards closed his editorial by saying, "the writings of Dr. Davies are not suitable for 'a mighty army marching forth to victory.' He sounds more like a drummer boy beating a retreat . . . . We believe that Southern Baptists cannot grow spiritually on a diet like Dr. Davies offers. I'm not prepared to 'eat it.' How about you?"

A week after Edwards' editorial the editor of *The Baptist Messenger* of Oklahoma wrote an editorial entitled "Warning to Our People." He, too, zeroed-in on Davies' handling of the Abraham-Isaac event. He said: "The book is a deep disappointment. Don't waste your money buying it. Don't waste your time reading it."

In the March 5, 1970 edition of the state Baptist paper of Tennessee, J. Wash Watts, former Professor of Hebrew and Old Testament at New Orleans Baptist Theological Seminary, wrote on "Conflicts Between the Treatment of Genesis in the Broadman Bible Commentary and the Bible Itself." Watts declared that Davies' interpretation of Genesis 22 "casts dark doubt on the word of the Bible." Rhetorically he asked, "Can Southern Baptists remain loyal to their confession of faith in the inspiration of the Bible and promote a treatment that abuses it as this one does?"

Just as Ralph Elliott had some support from Southern Baptists, so did the Broadman Commentary. "In Defense of the Broadman Bible Commentary" was the title of an editorial by C. R. Daley, Jr. in the Kentucky Baptist paper. "With Dr. Davies and his critics it is the same old story of literalism versus nonliteralism," Daley said. He pointed out that one could differ with Davies' interpretation of the Bible without accusing the scholar of denying the inspiration of the Bible. Daley also said that "the only way to satisfy every critic would be to let each critic write his own commentary." [11]

The Southern Baptist Convention met in Denver June 1–4. On May 30, just prior to the convention, a group of Southern Baptists met in what was called the "Affirming the Bible Conference." The announcement of such a conference was issued by Ross Edwards on March 12. He declared that a vocal minority of liberals had "challenged Bible-believing Baptists" ever since the 1962 Southern Baptist Convention in San Francisco. The conference on "Affirming the Bible" was called, according to Edwards, because "we want Southern Baptist liberals to know that there is a limit to our patience." [12] Some attributed what they called the noisy and militant Southern Baptist Convention of Denver to a negative influence issuing from this conference.

The motion which produced the most stir at the 1970 Southern Baptist Convention was presented by Gwin T. Turner of California. He moved "that because the new *The Broadman Commentary* is out of keeping with the beliefs of the vast majority of Southern Baptist pastors and people this Convention request the Sunday School Board to withdraw

Volume 1 from further distribution and that it be rewritten with due consideration of the conservative viewpoint." [13]

In his criticism of the commentary, Turner claimed that it directly contradicted the Bible. He referred specifically to the Abraham-Isaac sacrifice episode. James L. Sullivan, executive-secretary of the Sunday School Board, defended the publication of the book by saying (1) that no book produced by Broadman Press is considered to be the official position of the Southern Baptist Convention and (2) that the board produced books for various segments of Southern Baptists.

Clifton J. Allen, general editor of the commentary, pled with the messengers to the Denver Convention, "Let us pass on to the next generation a heritage of the open mind and open Bible, to understand and interpret it under the leadership of the Holy Spirit." The plea was in vain; the motion to withdraw and rewrite the commentary passed 5,394 to 2,-170.

Two months following the Southern Baptist Convention the elected members of the Sunday School Board met at Glorieta, New Mexico, August 11–13. In keeping with the request of the Southern Baptist Convention, the board voted by a two-to-one margin to withdraw volume 1 of the Broadman Commentary from distribution and sale. The Board also named a special committee to make suggestions for re-writing the commentary from a conservative viewpoint.

When the Sunday School Board met in Nashville in January 1971, the special committee recommended that the authors of the Genesis and Exodus sections of the commentary be asked to rewrite their material. An amendment to the committee's report was adopted which asked the authors to accept "the task of rewriting Volume 1 of the commentary with due consideration of the conservative viewpoint." The phrase "with due consideration of the conservative viewpoint" was a part of the motion adopted by the Denver convention in June, 1970.[14]

It looked like the commentary would be rewritten by the same authors. But not so, at least not for the Genesis commentary. Some Southern Baptists felt the Sunday School Board had not done what the Denver Convention asked. So at the St. Louis Convention in June, 1971 the following motion passed by a majority of 2,672 to 2,290: "That the Sunday School Board be advised that the vote of the 1970 Convention regarding the rewriting of Volume 1 of the Broadman Commentary has not been followed and that the Sunday School Board obtain another writer and proceed with the commentary according to the vote of the 1970 convention in Denver."

Several points need to be noted here. First of all, the Sunday School Board thought by getting Davies and Honeycutt to revise the commentary the convention action of 1970 was being followed. Second, it was obvious that the major area of concern was not the Exodus section of the volume but the Genesis portion. The motion adopted in St. Louis called for the Sunday School Board to "obtain another writer." This was an obvious reference to Davies, although even this fact was not spelled out in the 1971 motion. Third, while the messengers to the convention vetoed Davies as the author of the Genesis section of the commentary, the vote was close. It won by a 382 vote margin. In contrast, however, the motion to rewrite the commentary won by a 3,224-vote margin. A greater percentage of Southern Baptists felt free to vote for the rewriting than felt free to dictate to the Sunday

School Board how or who should do the rewriting. Yet, the majority still wanted a new writer.

The elected trustees of the Sunday School Board met in July at Ridgecrest, North Carolina, and the following motion was approved by a vote of 34–21:

In response to the action of the Southern Baptist Convention in St. Louis regarding Volume 1 of the Broadman Bible Commentary, we request and authorize the administration to seek to secure a new author for the commentary on the text of Genesis, also to report to the January meeting of the board the progress achieved and any developments or complications calling for further direction or authorization by the board.[15]

At the writing of this book that is where the Broadman Commentary Controversy stands. The administration of the Sunday School Board has been requested and authorized "to seek to secure" a new writer for the Genesis commentary.

III

An in-depth analysis of the Elliott and Broadman controversies would make an interesting comparative study. Some bright-eyed graduate student ought to jump on it! For one thing, both controversies were stimulated by diverse interpretations of Genesis. And in both controversies "liberals" and "conservatives" accepted and affirmed the Bible as God's Word. However "conservatives" claimed that to deny the historicity of biblical events (or to refuse to take the Bible literally) is the same as denying the Bible as the reliable Word of God. "Liberals," on the other hand, said the important thing about the Bible is its message, not its literary nature.

One of the obvious contrasts in these two controversies is that the 1962 Southern Baptist Convention refused to ban

Elliott's book, while the 1970 Convention voted overwhelmingly to request the Sunday School Board to withdraw the Broadman Commentary. Why? One can only guess and offer the guesses to others. One, some Southern Baptist leaders who were strongly opposed to Elliott were just as strongly opposed to banning Elliott's book. E. S. James, for example, editor of the Texas Baptist paper and staunch Elliott critic, described the 1962 motion to withdraw *The Message of Genesis* as "unnecessary," "extreme," and "coercive." Said James, "Let's have our agencies free to make decisions and let's criticize them if they make wrong ones." [16] That attitude prevailed in 1962 but not in 1970.

Secondly, the 1962 Convention was afflicted with only one explosive issue—the Elliott Controversy. But the 1970 Convention had two other trouble spots in addition to the Broadman argument. One of these was the furor which had erupted over the Atlanta Morality Seminar, sponsored by the Christian Life Commission of the Southern Baptist Convention. The second was a general concern on the part of some regarding the alleged "liberal" tendencies of the Sunday School and Training Union literature. In a sense, there were just too many fires for the influential leadership of the Convention to put out in 1970. The fact that there were several fires and not just one aggravated the atmosphere.

Three, in the Elliott Controversy, the issue could be personalized and focused on Ralph Elliott, a man employed by a Southern Baptist institution. But in the Broadman Controversy the issue could not be personalized; Henton Davies was an English Baptist. The result? In the first controversy the spotlight was on a man; in the second, a book. Yet, both controversies were at bottom biblical and theological.

NOTES

1. See Roy Jennings, "Ralph Elliott: Six Years After *The Message of Genesis*," (*Baptist Men's Journal*, April-May-June, 1968) p. 6.

2. For this statement see *The Baptist Standard*, February 7, 1962, *Baptist and Reflector*, February 8, 1962, *The Religious Herald*, February 15, 1962, and other state Baptist papers.

3. Salvador T. Martinez, "Southern Baptist Views of the Scriptures in Light of the Elliott Controversy," unpublished Th.M. thesis, Southern Baptist Theological Seminary, 1966, pp. 179, 180. Microfilm print, Dargan-Carver Library, Nashville.

4. For editorial positions on the Oklahoma Meeting see *The Baptist Standard*, May 30, 1962; *The Baptist Message*, March 15, 1962; and *Arkansas Baptist Newsmagazine*, March 22, 1962.

5. For a good discussion of the background and results of this recommendation, see Herschel H. Hobbs, *The Baptist Faith and Message* (Nashville: Convention Press, 1971) pp. 13–17.

6. *Southern Baptist Convention Annual*, 1962, pp. 65, 68.

7. See *Baptist Press* News Releases for October 28, 1962, and October 29, 1962, in Dargan-Carver Library, Baptist Sunday School Board, Nashville, Tennessee.

8. Davis C. Woolley, "Major Convention Crises Over a Century and a Quarter," *Review and Expositor*, Spring, 1970, p. 179.

9. James L. Sullivan, "Why the Broadman Commentary Was Published," (*Western Recorder*, April 11, 1970) p. 11.

10. G. Henton Davies, "Genesis," (*The Broadman Bible Commentary*, volume 1, 1969) p. 198.

11. See *Western Recorder*, April 11, 1970, p. 4.

12. *The Word and Way*, March 12, 1970, p. 2.

13. *Southern Baptist Convention Annual*, 1970, p. 63.

14. For a full report of this meeting of the Sunday School Board see *Baptist and Reflector*, February 4, 1971, p. 8.

15. See *Baptist Press* News Release, July 23, 1971.

16. See Martinez, *op. cit.*, pp. 28, 29.

Lessons from Baptist Controversies

The *facts* of history are not enough. We must learn the *lessons* of history, too. To make a denominational application: Baptists must do more than memorize the names, dates, and places of their yesterdays. We must learn the lessons which issue from the interaction of those hard-to-pronounce names, hard-to-remember dates, and hard-to-locate places. The study of history, as the study of the Bible, must be applied. In other words, there is a "so-what" element to the study of history.

Conflict and controversy have been at the very center of Baptist life. Indeed, I believe one could write a comprehensive and adequate denominational history if he focused only on the theme of controversy. Write a book entitled *Baptist Controversies,* and you have written a somewhat satisfactory summary of Baptist history. Baptists have squabbled from their very beginning—back in seventeenth-century England. They have argued over their history, their theology, their organization and church polity, the meaning of their ordinances, the missionary task of the church, and the social application of the gospel.

Throughout the chapters of the book I have tried to offer some interpretation of how the individual controversies have affected Southern Baptists. But in these closing pages an enumeration of a few of the more general lessons to be learned from Baptist controversies may be helpful.

Lesson Number One: Controversy is inevitable among Baptists. Baptist life is built upon basic democratic principles which not only allow controversy; they encourage it. There is a strong stubborn streak of individualism in Baptist life. Look at the concept of faith—it is individualistic and personal. Each man does his own repenting. Each man accepts God's grace personally. Each man comes "before God" on his own. Look at the concept of the church—each local congregation is free under Christ to run her own affairs. No outside organization, political or religious, can usurp the independence of the local church. Look at the aversion to creeds—only sacred Scriptures are normative for Baptists. We refuse to forfeit the freedom of biblical interpretation for the uniformity of any single theological statement. Look at the emphasis on religious liberty! On separation of church and state! On the priesthood of all believers!

These ideas scream for freedom and issue in variety. One great Baptist soul said: "The passion of the Baptists for liberty is one of their most strongly marked characteristics, flowing directly from the spiritual individualism which is their primary emphasis." [1] Individualism demands freedom. Freedom creates diversity. Diversity inevitably leads to controversy.

Baptists couldn't avoid controversy. It was built into our major emphases. If you begin where Baptists begin—with individualism and freedom—you are driven to where Baptists are driven—controversy and conflict. On the other hand, if you begin wanting theological and doctrinal sameness, if you are fearful of differences and painful conflict, you will have to look elsewhere than to Baptists.

While contemporary Baptists often are portrayed as a parochial and narrow-minded group, narrow-mindedness has not been one of the salient characteristics of the Baptist tradition. Baptists are not nearly so much like King Frederick of Austria as some would have us believe. It was said of the king that he loved music, but not all music, just music played on a flute; but not all music played on a flute, just the music played on his own flute; but not all music played on his own flute, just the music which he played on his own flute!

While some Baptists—both past and present—have doubtless enjoyed only that music which they play on their own flutes, Baptist heritage has not usually issued a call for that kind of dedication to narrowness. Flexibility is built into the Baptist way of doing things. That flexibility produces diversity and conflict.

Lesson Number Two: Controversy is painful but often profitable. No one has made this point any better than John Clifford (1836–1923), one of the giants of English Baptist history. In 1888, a time of great theological and doctrinal unrest among English Baptists, Clifford preached a historic sermon which confronted and exposed rather than ignored and white-washed the controversy. Clifford quoted another Baptist who said, " 'The evils of controversy are all temporary, and its benefits are all permanent.' " Then Clifford added, "It is a consolatory message. We accept it with thankfulness; but it remains 'a hard saying.' " [2]

So true. It is "a hard saying" because controversy is painful. During denominational controversy there have always been those who, like the false prophets of the Old Testament, predict "Peace, peace, when there is no peace." They are not really false prophets. They are honest men and women who want to detour pain by detouring controversy. But it can't be done—at least not always. For denominations, like little boys with leg-aches, have "growing pains." And they hurt. But it is better to hurt and grow than to never hurt and never grow.

Said John Clifford: "Controversy is far better than stagnation. Even strife is a sign of vitality—uncomfortable, irritating, perhaps; exceedingly disagreeable to fossil theologians and actual tyrants; but still it is vitality." And again: "He is not the typical Christian who is forever hugging the shores in search of the quited harbors, but he who braves the storm and tempest with his lifeboat that he may save." And again: "Living men differ. It is the dead who agree." And finally: "God educates His Church, if I may say it, by the Socratic method." [3]

Controversy has been exceedingly profitable for the Baptist denomination. The Whitsitt Controversy not only intensified interest in Baptist history, it delivered us from erroneous ideas. The controversy among English Baptists concerning the missionary responsibility of the churches launched the modern missionary movement, not just among Baptists but all religious bodies.

It is said that Mexican villagers who assume the worst is to be expected, often bid so-long to departing travelers with the blessing, "May you go with God, and may nothing new happen to you." Impossible! When people "go with God," new things happen. They are more often than not controversial and painful. And quite often they are profitable. So one should not pray that a denomination be delivered from all wrangling.

And yet, this is no call to embrace the new and novel indiscriminately. Nor is it a call to arms, thinking that if we do battle we shall "grow up" as a denomination. Wayne E. Oates wisely observed that either to deify or to deny the past has disastrous results for a person. And so with a denomination. Somehow we must learn to live in the terrible tension between what "was" and what "is."

Lesson Three: Controversy is often embodied in powerful personalities. This is true of controversy of any kind, but it is especially true of Baptist controversy. Because Baptists have refused to commit themselves to official creeds, authoritative church manuals, or ecclesiastical laws—things to which they could turn for final answers in a time of controversy—they have been left to follow the man with the eloquent voice, the power of persuasion, the genius of leadership, and/or the courage to voice a new conviction.

The power of personality is evident when one looks at the names of certain Baptist controversies. We have had the "Whitsitt" Controversy, the "Elliott" Controversy, the "Norris" Controversy. And even when the controversy did not assume the name of one of its central figures, one can hardly think of a Baptist conflict without thinking of certain names. Spurgeon is associated with the "Downgrade" Controversy, J. R. Graves with the "Landmark" Controversy, and Daniel Parker and John Taylor the "Anti-Missions" Controversy.

There is both a positive and a negative lesson here. The positive lesson is the fact that quite often very good and stalwart Christian leaders have advocated opposite points of view. Men differed because they honestly held divergent interpretations on an issue and not because they had "ulterior motives," lacked "integrity" or some such. But the negative lesson is the fact that controversy often degenerates into silly name-calling and demolishes the ministry and career of a good man. This has happened in Baptist history.

While controversy is most often embodied in powerful personalities, it should not become "personal." To label a person a "liberal," "fundamentalist," "radical," "activist" is too often an excuse for not using hard, critical thinking and a way of confessing that one lacks the patience to listen. Labels should be for identifying point of view; they are frequently used to accuse and indict. Our opinions may be wrong; our courtesy, fairness, and love will never be.

Lesson Four: A controversy is never finally and absolutely settled among Baptists. And for a very good reason; there is no person, persons, or organization from whom a final word can come in Baptist life. Baptists have often issued confessions of faith and public statements. These documents were directed toward a particular question. But they only indicated the point of view of a majority of Baptists at a particular time. These do not become binding on all Baptists. Baptists have consistently refused to be restricted by anything that smacked of creedalism.

One of the clearest examples of this attitude is to be found in the confession of faith adopted by the Southern Baptist Convention in 1925. The reason for the confession was "the prevalence of naturalism in the modern teaching" and specifically the idea of evolution. The committee which drafted and presented the confession of faith also presented a statement on the nature and functions of confessions of faith among Baptists. The committee said they did not regard confessional documents "as complete statements of our faith, having any quality of finality of infallibility." Moreover, "confessions are only guides in interpretation, having no authority over the conscience."

Occasionally you may hear a distraught Baptist say of a lingering denominational agitation, "Let's forget that argument, we settled that years ago." Rest assured that he is wrong. Nothing is ever finally and irrevocably settled among Baptists. This is part of the Baptist genius.

The above are four of the most obvious lessons from Baptist controversies. But one certainly cannot say, "Here endeth the lessons." The centrality of Baptist newspapers, the fact that theological controversy often is settled with the big stick of a financial boycott (the we'll-stop-giving syndrome), the fact that personality conflicts give rise to denominational disputes—these are just a few of the "other" lessons one could point to in Baptist controversies.

When you study Baptist history, you will understand that the old adage which says "anytime you find two Baptists you will find three ideas" is not far from true. The Baptist denominational consciousness has been fostered more by the unity which comes from a commitment to diversity than by the unity which comes from uniformity.

NOTES

1. H. Wheeler Robinson, *The Life and Faith of the Baptists* (London: Carey Kingsgate Press, Ltd., 1946) p. 123.

2. As quoted in Sydnor L. Stealey, *A Baptist Treasury* (New York: Thomas Y. Crowell Co., 1958) p. 98.

3. *Ibid.*, pp. 98–101.